READING THE WORLD
OF WORK

A Learner-Centered Approach to
Workplace Literacy and ESL

The Professional Practices in Adult Education and Lifelong Learning Series explores issues and concerns of practitioners who work in the broad range of settings in adult and continuing education and lifelong learning.

The books provide information and strategies on how to make practice more effective for professionals and those they serve. They are written from a practical viewpoint and provide a forum for instructors, administrators, policy makers, counselors, trainers, instructional designers, and other related professionals. The series contains single author or coauthored books only and does not include edited volumes.

Sharan B. Merriam
Ronald M. Cervero
Series Editors

READING THE WORLD OF WORK

A Learner-Centered Approach to Workplace Literacy and ESL

Melina L. Gallo

KRIEGER PUBLISHING COMPANY
MALABAR, FLORIDA
2004

Original Edition 2004

Printed and Published by
KRIEGER PUBLISHING COMPANY
KRIEGER DRIVE
MALABAR, FLORIDA 32950

FROM A DECLARATION OF PRINCIPLES JOINTLY ADOPTED BY A COM-
MITTEE OF THE AMERICAN BAR ASSOCIATION AND A COMMITTEE OF
PUBLISHERS:

This publication is designed to provide accurate and authoritative information in regard to the subject matter covered. It is sold with the understanding that the publisher is not engaged in rendering legal, accounting, or other professional service. If legal advice or other expert assistance is required, the services of a competent professional person should be sought.

Library of Congress Cataloging-in-Publication Data

Gallo, Melina L.
    Reading the world of work : a learner-centered approach to workplace
    literacy and ESL / Melina L. Gallo. — Original ed.
        p.   cm. — (Professional practices in adult education and lifelong
        learning series)
    Includes bibliographical references (p.) and index.
    ISBN 1-57524-217-6 (alk. paper)
    1. Workplace literacy—United States. 2. Student-centered learning—
    United States—3. English language—Study and teaching—United
    States—Foreign speakers. I. Title. II. Series.
    LC151.G35 2004
    374′.0124—dc22   2003062081

10   9   8   7   6   5   4   3   2

For my parents, Robert and Beverly Gallo

CONTENTS

PREFACE

This book hopes to change notions of what it means to be literate in the workplace, to enlighten and educate practitioners about creative approaches to learning, and to help workplace literacy programs reach their potential as a positive means of educating workers and transforming the world of work. It describes inventive ways of learning and teaching that go beyond traditional expectations to engage workers in meaningful communication and change-making. Workplace literacy programs can become more effective by implementing a learner-centered approach to aid language learning through problem posing and critical thinking. By using learners' own experiences and current needs, educators can provide a common ground for adults of differing language backgrounds and learning styles to better manage the literacies in a workplace culture. Additionally, we can help workers learn to negotiate and change the environment of their workplace, to find ways of expanding their opportunities and expertise rather than whittling themselves down to fit into a predetermined slot. The ideas guiding these approaches are based in Paulo Freire's theories of critical literacy, in which learners are active creators rather than passive recipients of knowledge.

There is a pressing need to make information about workplace literacy alternatives accessible to a variety of adult educators including reading practitioners, program developers, ESL instructors, HRD professionals, and policy makers. As a long-time workplace basic skills instructor, I am familiar with the challenges of teaching in factory cafeterias and railroad yard trailers, working at odd hours to reach workers on the midnight shift, and dealing with the often conflicting needs of learners and employers. I became frustrated with trying to use conventional instructional materials and methods that did not acknowledge the realities of my students and began to develop approaches to literacy education that work at work. Such a wide chasm exists between academic theoreticians and the workplace educators in the trenches that I sometimes find it difficult to explain critical literacy to my colleagues working in the field who don't see what ESL and basic skills have to do with critical awareness or multiple literacies, let alone social justice and humanization of the workplace. This book offers practical insights into some of the issues and effective approaches in workplace literacy programs that will be helpful to all involved in planning and delivering these programs. We cannot prepare workers for a continuously changing and technologically advanced workforce by using the old teaching techniques that have emphasized rote memorization, discrete skills, and assimilation into the existing work order. Instead, learning that emphasizes critical thinking, problem posing, and creativity is needed.

This book helps to explain the conflicting dynamics inherent in many workplace literacy programs as well as offering alternative approaches to learning which are empowering for workers. It shows how the lofty ideals of seeking justice and dignity have a place among the gritty realities of profit, production, and pronunciation in the workplace. It describes ways that business and human interest can intersect to create educational programs that are good for organizations and their workers and argues that even in uncertain economic climates where reality seemingly limits workers' options to the lesser of the evils, clinging onto a bad job versus facing unemployment, there is still room for a pedagogy of hope.

While numerous guides are available that prescribe formulaic procedures and techniques for programs based upon learners' deficits, there are few books which assist adult educators in implementing the possibilities of learner-centered workplace literacy programs centered on workers' strengths. Companies that recognize the benefits of supporting on-site literacy programs will find that this book explains specific approaches and practices which can be effective in engaging adult learners in learning to read and navigate their work worlds. It addresses questions such as, What do employers expect of their employees' literacy? What do workers want and need to learn? What does society want from adult literacy programs? Should workplace education domesticate or emancipate? Does it only offer the limited hope of aiding workers in keeping their current low skill jobs or is it a stepping-stone to greater opportunities and possibilities? And how can the world of work become more equitable?

Chapter 1, "The Politics and Promise of Workplace Literacy," introduces some of the current issues. While employers may want an increasingly high skilled workforce to compete in a globalized and technologically advancing marketplace, they are often reluctant to pay the higher wages such skilled workers demand. Instead, by providing on-site literacy instruction to their current employees, organizations seek to upgrade the skills of their workforce. Workers targeted for literacy training are usually immigrants or working class Americans with limited education. They may work in jobs with little security and few benefits which frequently pay less than a living wage. However, conventional workplace literacy classes too often do little to change their current work situations or future opportunities. Instead workers are given minimal training by methods that can actually hinder rather than help their advancement. Critical learning can benefit both employers and workers in ways that strict, short-sighted adherence to traditional training does not.

The second chapter, "Expanding Definitions of Literacies and Learning," explains the problems inherent in traditional instructional techniques in the workplace and describes differing literacies and learning approaches including literacy for specific workforce skills, the deficit approach to literacy instruction, and critical approaches to literacy. The values transmitted to working-class learners typically emphasize skills such as following directions, rote memorization, and punctuality, rather than the opportunities to practice critical thinking, creativity, and leadership. Using learners' stories, visual images, and workplace change projects as a common base of communication can be a positive way of dealing with language, culture, and learning preference differences.

The third chapter describes the steps to start a program including identifying needs, evaluating the company culture, and garnering support from all involved parties. Investigating the current communicative practices and spoken and unspoken program expectations are essential parts of this phase. The role of the adult educator in educating management on literacy and learning, and advocating for workers is also described. Balancing the often-conflicting desires of learners, funding providers, management, and unions are considered. Ways of finding appropriate class times, instructional space, and compensation for workers involved are also included.

The fourth chapter involves both learners and their co-workers in improving the communicative practices throughout the workplace. This includes strategies such as critically reading workplace texts, valuing cultural and communicative differences, and engaging coworkers outside the class as mentors and co-learners. Successful ways of integrating foreign language instruction and cultural awareness are recommended. By involving learners in workplace improvement projects from writing suggestions and speaking up at meetings to rewriting company documentation in clear English, educators can provide opportunities for learners to immediately use their new literacy skills in authentic situations.

Chapter 5 explains ways of engaging learners through sharing of their own stories and experiences. Dialogue journals, codifications, discussions of work experiences, and guest speakers from the company and community may be included as valuable learning resources. This section focuses on learners' immediate literacy needs in and out of work by offering requested lessons such as helping children with homework, writing checks, or completing bureaucratic forms.

The sixth chapter describes the use of visual imagery including drawing, photography, video, and other multi-media expressions as tools for creating a learner-centered curriculum. Suggestions for building class activities around photography and transferring learning outside of the classroom are detailed. It also discusses the act of photographing as empowerment and describes the ways in which learners can begin to critically reflect upon the invisible realm of the workplace, by freezing everyday images and uncovering their themes. Exhibiting galleries of workers' images within the company, creating murals, publishing booklets of learners' photo-essays, and utilizing the Internet are powerful methods of displaying the knowledge learners have made.

The final chapter discusses program assessment that goes beyond standardized test scores. Barriers and bridges to transferring learning from the classroom to the workplace are explored. Additionally, documenting workplace transformations and providing venues for learners to share accounts of their successes serve as important evaluation tools. Ways of implementing workplace improvement projects and showing financial benefits to the organization through improved safety, productivity, and diminished turnover are also included. It is valuable to recognize and publicize the widespread ways that the organization, workers, and community alike may benefit in the return on investment from these programs.

I hope that this book will contribute to the field of workplace literacy by providing inventive and practical approaches to becoming literate about the world of work that can be customized for the unique situations found in an array of organizations. It shows program planners how to help workplace literacy programs to reach their full potential by actively creating supportive working and learning environments and listening to the voices of the workers themselves.

ACKNOWLEDGMENTS

This book would not be possible without the help and guidance of many others. I would first like to express my gratitude to Laurie Elish-Piper, who has been with me from the beginning of this project which began in her Adult Reading Instruction course and whose boundless enthusiasm and insights have encouraged me to explore the possibilities of workplace literacy. I also wish to thank the other members of my dissertation committee from Northern Illinois University for their suggestions and encouragement: Phyllis M. Cunningham, who was a wonderful chair, bolstering my confidence and keeping me on track; and Jorge Jeria, who introduced me to the ideas of Freire in my first adult education course and inspired me to continue my studies. Phyllis suggested that I submit my dissertation for publication which I naively thought would involve a few minor rewrites. Instead this book emerged as a very different text. Many thanks to my editors Ron Cervero and Sharan Merriam for their expertise in guiding me through this project from the proposal stage and their encouragement and thoughtful help with revisions and to Mary Roberts and Joyce M. Parks for their support and insights in the final edits. Thanks are also due to my colleague Peggy Fergus who kindly read the manuscript and offered her own valuable professional experiences.

I also wish to thank Phyllis Ham Garth and all the participants who offered their ideas and critiques in the monthly meetings of the Live Poet's group. Special thanks also go to my great friend and reference librarian, Carole Svensson, who helped me find elusive sources of information and delve through endless statistics. I owe a great debt to the outstanding service of librarian Mary Ellen Krasula who tirelessly lugged library books from the main campus to my office and patiently answered my reference questions.

Words cannot express the gratitude I have for my amazing family, especially my husband, Johnny Lukashevich, my parents, Robert and Beverly Gallo, and my sister Tracy Gallo, whose ongoing love and support sustain me and bring me joy. I am also grateful to share my life with Sandy, Ralph, and Alex Blust; Agnes, Patricia, Dennis, Jeanie, and David Gallo; Lorinda, Dean, Jessica, Katie, and Lindsey Grilli; Debbie and Tommy Iorio; Tony Sr., Arlene, Tony Jr., Sue, and Zoe Lukashevich; and Pat Saharsky who keep me afloat with their unceasing help, humor, and love.

Additional thanks go out to all my friends at Faith Church for all of their prayers and blessings, and to Lisa Bergman who bravely risked the well-being of her own computer to save my unwieldy files. Further thanks are due to Elsa Auerbach, Adell Newman, Randy Pierson, and Kjell Rubensen for answering important questions. Finally, I would like to thank my students who have patiently endured my growth as a teacher and shared their lives and learning with me.

THE AUTHOR

Melina L. Gallo teaches and designs curriculum through Northern Illinois University's Business and Industry Services. She has taught workplace ESL, literacy, and numeracy in more than 40 companies including 3M and General Motors. She also teaches on a variety of other workplace subjects including technical writing, Spanish, and computer skills. She earned her doctorate in Adult Education from Northern Illinois University and her Master's degree in Linguistics with a concentration in teaching ESL from Northeastern Illinois University. Her award-winning research in the field of workplace communication has been presented and published internationally.

CHAPTER 1

The Politics and Promise of Workplace Literacy

Striking a balance between mere work skill training and transformative education, between academic theorizing and the realities of people with limited literacy struggling to keep their jobs, between the rhetoric of government and business and the language of the shop floor is the newly emerging and uncharted field of workplace literacy. Workplace educators find themselves caught in the midst of political and moral dilemmas, as they struggle to frame their work in a way that appeases those who are paying for classes and appeals to those that are participating in them. While many employers claim to be seeking a more highly skilled workforce (National Association of Manufacturers, 2002), they are often reluctant to offer the greater wages commensurate with such skills. Instead, by providing on-site literacy instruction to their employees, companies propose to improve the skills of their current workforce as well as productivity and profitability.

Workplace literacy, often called basic skills, programs offer the promise of helping workers with low literacy skills or limited English proficiency to improve their education through accessible programs. It is a practical solution to reaching and educating disadvantaged adults in the places where they are and for the most relevant reasons. Workplace literacy programs are becoming an increasingly important, though at times controversial, means of educating workers today. These programs have been praised by some as a solution to improving a flagging economy in an era of global competitiveness. The programs are condemned as doing too little by others, who view them as mere public relations ploys that serve to individualize societal problems. At present, it is estimated that about 20%–30% of large U.S. workplaces are engaged in providing some type of basic skills training for their employees (Boyle, 2001). Employers who wish to bolster the skills of their current workforce offer literacy programs on site providing basic skills training including English as a second language (ESL), reading, and math. These programs are usually paid for by a combination of private and public funds and concentrate on training workers in the specific skills required for their work.

The issues of workplace literacy are increasingly important as the nation's focus on literacy instruction for the purposes of employment is increasing and more funds are being diverted from school, community, and family-based literacy programs to workforce programs. While the field of workplace literacy continues to grow and evolve, it is vital to foster an understanding of the dynamics inherent in these programs and offer improved approaches to educating learners about the literacy skills needed in the workplace. Simplistic assumptions that education will lead to better employment opportunities, that learners must pull themselves up by their own bootstraps, and that employers will reward skilled workers must be investigated. There is little literature that provides assistance to adult educators dealing critically with the challenges and opportunities of the workplace literacy classroom in the United States. Most workplace literacy instruction is not learner-centered and therefore has limited effectiveness in engaging learners and improving their literacy skills. A learner-centered approach to workplace literacy is an innovative means of instruction that uses learners' own strengths, concerns, and interests as the starting point for building their language and literacy skills. It helps workers not only in reading words, but also in learning how to navigate the power dynamics and culture of the workplace by reading the world of work.

The differences in the ways that employers and educators define terms such as *critical thinking*, *empowerment*, and *literacy* can be a source of conflict or a space for expanding understanding and possibilities. While employers often state that they want to empower their workers to take responsibility for their jobs, speak up about ways of implementing continuous improvement, and become more successful, there are frequently very narrow spaces in which this responsibility, speaking, and success are considered appropriate. There may be a perceived risk to employers that workers will learn too much, that they will demand better wages and work conditions, that they will challenge authority with the newfound knowledge and self-confidence gained through their learning (Boyle, 2001).

Many politicians and educators have touted workplace literacy programs as the panacea for economic uncertainty in this postindustrial age of information (Ford, 1992; Ryan, 1994). Better skilled workers will ensure greater productivity and economic security as North America competes in the global marketplace, the argument goes, though thousands of jobs are being lost overseas to even lower skilled and lower wage workers. Innovative companies initiate Continuous Improvement, Total Quality, and Learning Organization systems which pay lip service to the concepts of employee empowerment, teamwork, and shared vision while too often simultaneously slashing job security and wages. The contradictions inherent in these policies are largely ignored by the many players in the workplace literacy arena. These include politicians, corporations, and educational providers, all of whom have incentives for exaggerating the extent and effects of illiteracy in the workplace. There is a widespread suspicion that rampant worker illiteracy is to blame for a sundry list of workplace woes including poor production, high turnover, and inferior-quality job performance. This belief in workers' deficits is central to many workplace literacy policies. The idea that illiterate (and therefore incompetent) workers are to blame for loss of economic competitiveness, as well as their own problems, is a popularly held belief (Hull, 1997b). Through this cacophony of ominous warnings about the dangers of illiteracy, the voice of the worker is rarely heard.

THE BENEFITS OF WORKPLACE LITERACY PROGRAMS

Workplace literacy programs provide many benefits and positive outcomes. Employers reap many economic, organizational, and even social rewards by providing basic skills classes. Employers may expect that by improving workers' skills they will improve productivity, safety, and quality as well. Organizations also seek increased profitability, reduced absenteeism, tax write-offs and greater customer satisfaction. Other reasons given for implementing basic skills programs include public relations, opportunities for retaining or promoting current employees, and a higher rate of employee success in further training. Many organizations also report better morale and improved labor relations. Literacy education allows organizations to express their humane values, commitment, and loyalty to employees. Boyle (2001) states that these programs can foster equality and cultural understanding and may serve as a safety valve where "the teachers explicitly teach about cultural differences . . . so that the literacy class offers a place to address ethnic, racial, and even working class tension in the workplace." (p. 99). She also points out that employers have changed their explanations for offering literacy programs over the years by variously citing such reasons as Americanization, affirmative action, and better utilization of technology.

Though most companies offer some type of job-related training, it is disproportionately doled out to college-educated employees. Too often the workers who need the most education and could most benefit from the chance to increase their skills are also the least likely to have training opportunities. This widens the gap between skilled and unskilled workers. Offering basic skills classes to less educated workers is a step toward narrowing this chasm and allowing workers to access further education. Many employers wish to be good corporate citizens in their communities, and these programs allow them to attract new workers as well as retaining those they have already hired. Avoiding the accidents and errors that can be made from the inability to read instructions and improving the communications skills to help workers deal more ably with customers, coworkers, and the public are additional goals cited by many organizations (Canadian Labour Congress, 2000).

Workplace literacy also offers great advantages for learners who participate in the programs. Beyond the ordinary intrinsic and extrinsic rewards associated with other types of adult basic education (ABE) programs such as improved self-esteem and job opportunities, workplace literacy education provides some unique benefits. The convenience of the scheduling and location of programs as well as the opportunity (in many cases) to be paid for their time in class makes it an unparalleled educational opportunity for low-wage workers. These are laborers who often work long hours, either holding down more than one job or working overtime in order to meet their basic needs, and may lack the time and resources necessary to travel to classes after work hours (Hull, 1997a).

Another positive aspect of these programs is the inclusion of job-related subject matter that is relevant to their work and more likely to be useful in their daily lives than the content of generic ABE classes. Many immigrants speak their first languages at home and may shop, worship, and socialize largely within their own ethnic language communities. For these language learners, the workplace is their primary site for English usage; learning the vocabulary and customs characteristic to this environment is essential. Many U.S.-born nonreaders have also built a social system in which others help them with reading and writing and they have structured their lives to avoid unfamiliar situations in which difficult texts may be encountered. These tactics ensure that their limited reading skills are rarely felt as a deficit. In the workplace however, changing job duties and the introduction of new technology may make the need to read and write inescapable. For these learners, the workplace, with its industry-specific vocabulary and documents, becomes the logical and optimal place for literacy classes to occur. Filling out accident report forms, negotiating with supervisors, reading contracts, and understanding customer requests are the essential areas where many workers want to improve their communication skills. The workplace becomes an excellent place to learn, precisely because it offers so many relevant opportunities for communication.

Women who have been denied education opportunities by their partners or families can also benefit from these programs by participating clandestinely or without blame (Gowen &

Bartlett, 1997). Additionally, there are indications that workers feel more prepared to participate in further workplace training and to cope with job changes when they have improved their basic skills. They can better understand health and safety regulations and employee benefits, and they may feel more confident in expressing their suggestions at work. All of these factors combine to make workplace literacy programs potentially one of the most accessible, relevant, and effective means of educating adults.

In addition to the clear-cut benefits to employers and workers who participate in these programs, there are additional rewards to society as a whole, which are not always as clearly articulated. Parents who can read, do math, use computers, and understand English are more likely to be able to help their children with homework and participate in school activities and educational meetings. Communities that have a higher percentage of literate residents may have more active civic participation as well as lower rates of unemployment and crime. An educated citizenry is better able to make informed decisions when voting for candidates or issues (Thorn, 2001). Research shows compelling arguments for increasing the support given to workplace literacy programs. Employer sponsored adult education has the potential to be a widespread solution to meeting the needs of employers, workers, and society by filling the need for accessible literacy education.

WHO IS RESPONSIBLE FOR WORKERS' EDUCATION?

Given the wide range of positive outcomes to workplace literacy programs, we may wonder why more companies are not providing basic skills classes. Part of the reason may be that employers do not see this as their responsibility. They are in the business of business and the burden of educating their workers might well be viewed as someone else's obligation.

It is not clear who has the primary responsibility for educating workers. Is it the government, the employers, or the workers? Who benefits from workplace education? Is it in society's interest to have a well-educated citizenry? What responsibility do employers have for the safety or future of the low literate workers they recruit? Is literacy a privilege or a right? While governments in other countries such as the U.K. have made adult literacy education a funding priority, in the United States it is a crazy quilt made up of volunteers, faith-based organizations, community colleges, community groups, businesses, unions, foundations, and governmental initiatives, trying with limited resources to meet the needs of low literate adults. As Boyle points out:

> No sector has a clear mandate for solving the illiteracy problem . . . Employers want to train in work skills, not basic reading and writing. Volunteers have little visibility and episodic tolerance for the politics . . . unions represent only a fraction of the illiterate adults, and have more pressing global concerns. The adults themselves, unorganized with limited English proficiency, are hardly a powerful constituency. Adult educators have emerged as the champions of illiterate adults and literacy education, yet they must operate in a remarkably politicized environment. (p. 33).

Concern is growing that vocational literacy is displacing the funding of programs with wider goals (Fingeret & Drennon, 1997). Even the GED test, long used as a measure of basic educational attainment, has been recently redesigned to better meet the needs of employers. Learners who want to improve their reading in order to be able to read the newspaper or religious texts, help their children with homework, or better participate in the political system will find little relevance in vocationally focused programs. Some fear that the ever-encroaching field of workforce training will subsume the field of adult education, allowing corporations to limit and control the educational opportunities available for many people (Cunningham, 1993). These concerns can be addressed by encouraging individual workers to have input into the skills and education they would like to gain instead of just teaching what the employer thinks they should learn. This type of learner-centered curriculum ensures that learning which is funded with public tax dollars does not become just another form of corporate welfare providing nontransferable, dull, and ineffective training.

UNIQUE CHARACTERISTICS OF WORKPLACE LITERACY PROGRAMS

The cultural setting of a workplace literacy program may be very different than community or family-based literacy programs. Though the purpose of the classes is ostensibly to improve the literacy of the learners, programs are usually funded and set up by employers whose primary interests lie in improving profitability and productivity. The narrow approaches of much workplace curricula meet primarily the needs of the employers (Rose, 1992) rather than participatory program structures which suit the needs of learners both inside the workplace and outside. Because such classes are often mandatory, and learners may feel that their jobs are at risk if they do not participate appropriately, they are sometimes hesitant to speak freely or acknowledge difficult topics.

A popular belief is that "what is good for the employer is good for the employee—to be more productive and flexible, to define self in terms of work and to seek advancement in the system" (Gowen, 1992, p. 37). However, workers do not always embrace the same values as management. Instead of programs being relevant to workers' need of learning how to negotiate power in the workplace by reading the world of work, many programs are focused more on the literacy demands made by company management of adherence to written rules and procedures (Fingeret, 1994; O'Connor, 2000).

The workplace literacy educator's role is a precarious one, with most practitioners working part-time, often pulling together several piecemeal small jobs without benefits or long-term security. Paid hourly, and dependent on soft-money grants that can dry up as quickly as management whims, once they have managed to land a job, most educators are loath to stir up trouble by using unconventional teaching methods. They struggle daily to balance the need to meet funders' testing requirements and employers' expectations while satisfying the important learning needs of the workers themselves. Between these constraints on their own job security and learners' initial resistance to engaging in unfamiliar participatory learning practices, educators may easily become little more than a tool for producing marginally more literate workers without improving their prospects for a better future.

Boyle (1999) suggests that adult educators are divided in their support of workplace literacy. While some believe the workplace is the ideal setting for those who cannot access outside schooling, others believe that the employers' purposes will prevent liberatory or critical education, and programs will benefit only the organization, not the workers. Nevertheless, an uneasy partnership has sprung up between adult educators and businesses for the purposes of workplace literacy. The tradeoffs of learner-centeredness and critical approaches in exchange for the access and much needed financial support provided by business seem fair to many literacy providers. Though business may appear to be an ally of literacy educators with many overlapping interests, motives may differ. It is important that a balance be kept between learners' and management's interests, particularly when programs are funded by public grants. The needs of corporations are not always identical or even compatible with the needs of the people. Though we may need jobs, we do not *only* need jobs. Training focused solely on the needs of the current job market is short-sighted. Critical-thinking skills, communication skills, and decision-making skills all are necessary in addition to form filling and technical skills.

Workers are often skeptical about the claim that improving their literacy skills alone will provide opportunities for advancement. They are all too aware of the roles politics, age, and race play in the allotment of promotions (Gowen, 1992). The naïve idea that traditional literacy instruction will significantly improve advancement opportunities for participants operates in sharp contrast to the realities of racism, classism, sexism, favoritism, and other barriers in the workplace, which are well recognized by employees. Instructional providers as well as management encourage workers to "buy into" the exaggerated hopes of improved job opportunities and advancement in exchange for improved English and reading skills. Boyle (2001) even suggests that some workplace literacy programs may be largely symbolic, allowing employers to appear benevolent and committed to existing employees while at the same time sending the message that these illiterate workers are deserving of their current status.

WHO IS CONSIDERED "ILLITERATE" AND BY WHOM?

A shocking number of U.S. workers are reported to be functionally illiterate. These numbers range greatly but it is often reported that as many as 50% of adults in the United States read below a level 3 on the National Adult Literacy Survey (Sum, Kirsch, & Taggart, 2002). In the workplace, functional illiteracy may be a judgment call made by supervisors based on their employees' job performance skills rather than test scores. Some researchers (Boyle, 2001; Gilmore, 1992; Gowen, 1992; Shannon, 1992) have suggested that what is described as a literacy deficit is actually a race or class specific behavior that is viewed by supervisors as offensive because it differs from middle-class norms. Nonstandard uses of language whether black English, Spanish, or working-class slang are sometimes discouraged because they represent a threatening language of solidarity that cannot be fully controlled or understood by outsiders, only sporadically suppressed through "English only" policies and educational attempts at eradication. Groups including African Americans, Appalachians, and Latinos born in the United States are sometimes ostracized when their spoken English, gestures, and writing differs from that of the dominant culture. These workers may be characterized as "illiterate" by virtue of who they are and how they act, rather than what they know.

Literacy skill training alone is not sufficient to eliminate such inequities. Roberts, Davies, and Jupp (1992) found that immigrant workers who had participated in language training and improved their communications skills were still relegated to the lowest paying and most unpleasant jobs. They argue that workplace communication is connected to power issues and used to discriminate and exclude those who are not fluent in standard English. This prevents these workers from achieving equity and isolates them in undesirable jobs away from middle-class workers, which prevents them from further improving their communication skills. In this way, workplace discrimination can be deflected from race, ethnicity, and class issues by focusing instead on alleged communicative incompetence and illiteracy.

Excluding people who do not speak standard English from education opportunities under the guise of "standards" is another gatekeeping technique which may limit employment possibilities. These practices track people into dead-end jobs based on their class, race, gender, or ethnicity instead of opening doors and providing opportunities. Remaining silent allows these commonplace practices to continue. Workplace educators have the chance "to direct their practice towards the emancipation of learners rather than their renewed servitude" (Bouchard, 1998, p. 138) and have the opportunity to address these injustices through their work.

IMMIGRANTS AND LOW-LITERATE AMERICANS: SIMILARITIES AND DIFFERENCES

Low-skilled workers are still in great demand today. While much press is given to the high-paying, high-tech jobs in the workforce, the largest number of new jobs are actually being created in the low-skilled, low-wage service sector (Bureau of Labor Statistics, 2001a). Jobs available in other industries such as manufacturing are similarly biased toward work that requires relatively little formal education. These positions are often filled by immigrants or U.S.-born workers with low reading skills. Many employers sponsor workplace literacy programs that are created primarily for English as second language learners. Unlike Canada and the U.K., which differentiate between second language and literacy programs, in the United States they are often lumped together under "workplace literacy" or "basic skills," perhaps in order to draw attention away from the non-native workforce in an anti-immigrant political climate. This however, leads to confusion for some employers who group English speakers with reading difficulties along with non-English speakers into the same courses. While both groups share the burden of coping with insufficient literacy skills and being relegated to jobs at the bottom of the employment barrel, their educational needs and experiences are often very different.

Immigrants currently make up at least 13% of the U.S. workforce (Bureau of Labor Statistics, 2001b). Historically, immigrant laborers have toiled in the lowest paying and least desirable jobs in the United States, yet they still face discrimination and hostility from some Americans who believe they are lowering wages and taking jobs away from people born in this country (Beck, 1996; Reimers, 1998). Many immigrants may also have limited literacy in their first languages, which makes acquiring reading and writing skills in a new language particularly difficult. Even so, second language learners often are enthusiastic about the opportunity to expand their language skills and see obvious advantages to improving their English. They may value education highly and volunteer readily for English classes. Low-literate Americans, on the other hand, often have had very negative educational experiences in their past and do not see benefits in these classes. Nor are they eager to open the old wounds and unpleasant memories of previous academic inadequacy and failure (Quigley, 1993).

While employers may decry their workers' lack of skills, these low-literate workers are actually sought out and valued for their willingness to work hard at boring, demeaning, or grueling labor for the lowest wages: work their more skilled counterparts shun. Roberts, Davies, and Jupp (1992) point out that the jobs available to immigrants often offer very poor working conditions, close supervision, undesirable shift hours, low pay, extreme heat or cold, standing, monotony, and danger from exposure to chemicals and machinery. These are jobs which few very literate white Americans would accept.

Many undocumented workers come to the United States to serve business interests as a low-cost and easily disposable workforce. They are unlikely to organize, complain about unfair and inhumane work conditions, or demand pay raises. They are routinely let go when they become sick, are injured on the job, or are no longer needed without the costly workers' compensation insurance and unemployment benefits demanded by "legal" workers. The government can regulate the influx of these workers by cracking down on border patrol and deportation when the demand for immigrants' labor is lower and easing up when more cheap labor is desired. This readily available workforce is ideal for employers in most aspects except the workers' lack of English language and technical skills. Traditional workplace literacy training provides incremental English improvement without substantially bettering the workers' own conditions and opportunities. In contrast, learner-centered literacy education serves workers' interests as well by helping them to see systemic barriers, pose problems, and make changes in their circumstances.

BARRIERS TO TRADITIONAL METHODS OF TEACHING WORKPLACE LITERACY

While many progressive companies offer literacy classes as a positive way to improve opportunities for their workforce, traditionally designed basic skills classes are sometimes viewed as punitive or remedial. "If you fail the test, you'll just have to keep taking this class again and again until you pass," a human resource manager once warned my reading class. This attitude reinforces workers' perceptions that they are disempowered, much like children back in the school classroom. If not properly implemented, literacy programs can be threatening because they call attention to workers' educational shortcomings, instead of their job performance strengths. Unlike training provided for management, basic skills training is often associated with anxiety-provoking pre- and post-examinations and monotonous drills. Additionally, the items chosen by companies to be incorporated in the literacy classes may be viewed by learners as punitive, dull, or insulting. These frequently include items such as lists of work rules, written warning forms, absentee policies, and standard operating procedures. Such content offers few incentives for volunteers to join or remain in classes. This leads many companies to require mandatory literacy training for targeted employees, which elicits predictably negative attitudes toward the programs.

Deficit approaches to workplace literacy may foster the illusion of opportunity that disguises systemic barriers of discrimination and even enables them to persist (Boyle, 2001). It can promote docile acceptance of the status quo and lead learners to view themselves, rather than the system, as defective. Such programs can set up learners to be unsuccessful and to internalize the shortcomings of the program as their own failings. By promoting the assumption that everyone has an equal opportunity to make it, those who do not succeed in the work world can be categorized as lazy, incompetent, or dumb (Barndt, 1980). Workers who cannot learn to read or speak English fluently in 40 hours of training may feel as if it is their own fault, rather than a program shortcoming. No matter that foreign language learning typically takes years, not weeks, and that reading skills built upon deciphering work forms are unlikely to result in the sophisticated language required for promotions. The message sent may be that low-level workers are deserving of their current status and conditions and that opportunities for betterment have been offered and declined (Boyle, 2001).

Perhaps the most significant barrier to success in traditional programs is that workers themselves are almost never consulted during program planning and curriculum development. Educational providers and company management are usually the only parties involved. Even programs involving unions do not include significant learner involvement in these areas (Chaney, 1994). This exclusion of the primary participants during program design and implementation naturally leads to distrust and suspicion of the program being foisted upon them.

Another pitfall is workplace literacy programs that focus on the deficiencies of a group of employees to the exclusion of the communicative shortcomings found throughout the organization. While it is often assumed that an inability to read or speak the language is the only barrier to fluent and appropriate uses of literacy at work, workers may at times deliberately resist or be externally prevented from using their language skills. In many cases, there are deterrents for workers to read and speak in ways that the employer deems appropriate. Lack of opportunity to use new language skills on the job, poorly written company texts, and resistance to authority are some of the reasons workers may not display at work all the literate behaviors they possess. Low literate workers are also often segregated into "literacy-proofed" jobs where there are few opportunities to practice reading, writing, or speaking skills.

Workers may also lose literacy skills during adulthood. Being relegated to jobs that do not allow them to exercise their reading, writing, and math skills may actually rob workers of the ability to function in these areas. Unused skills atrophy quickly and people who read fairly well in high school may no longer be as comfortable doing so after 30 years away from text-rich environments. Jobs which provide few opportunities for new learning and exercising of skills disadvantage the workers within them, and those learning new skills find few opportunities to practice them in "literacy-proofed" jobs (Gowen, 1992).

A large barrier for workers with limited literacy is the texts that are found in the workplace. Company documentation is often encoded in a baffling blend of legalese and technical obfuscations that confound even the most educated and experienced readers. Though the very lives of workers depend upon their ability to read the safety instructions about handling dangerous chemicals found on Material Safety Data Sheets (MSDS), the terminology used, such as "carcinogenic" and "fetotoxic," is unlikely to be understood by the average manufacturing worker (Szudy & Arroyo, 1994). The use of such difficult language may be interpreted as a complete disregard for the audience to whom they are writing, a display of their power used to confuse and humiliate the less educated, or even a deliberate attempt to withhold information. Purcell-Gates (1995) refers to such practices as "exclusionary written language style."

In contrast to the suggestion implicit in the label "basic skills," the acquisition of fluency in a foreign language as an adult is a very high-order achievement that few people are able to accomplish. The expectations of the workplace, that limited-English-proficient workers and U.S.-born workers with minimal education and literacy skills should be expected to read documentation such as chemical information sheets written at a college-graduate level, are thoughtless at best and negligent or even intentionally misleading at worse.

Gowen (1992) found that in many cases refusal to read or carry out written directions at work was not a result of illiteracy but rather an act of resistance. Taking a stance against English-only policies or written communication requirements that workers find disrespectful to their talents and commonsense can be misinterpreted as illiteracy. Not all undesirable work behavior stems from inability to read the rules, though managers and workers alike may have interests in blaming lack of literacy or English skills for workplace problems.

WHOSE PURPOSES ARE SERVED?

The largest gains reported by many employers providing basic skill programs are not workers' advancement within the organization or even reading level improvements but rather the raising of "employee morale," perhaps a euphemism for the creation of more compliant and agreeable workers. These workplace literacy programs may merely serve as symbolic undertakings toward opportunity, the cooling out of workers' ambitions while transferring the responsibility of advancement and education to an individualized rather than organizational or societal model (Boyle, 2001). If workers succeed through such programs, the company takes the credit; if they fail, it is seen as their own fault. Because such programs seldom offer enough instructional time to make a significant difference in learners' skills, it suggests that the employers have little interest in doing so. In fact, many employers do not wish to pay the wages demanded by literate workers nor do they need them. Beyond the desire to appear benevolent, by offering a second chance for self-improvement to those who squandered their original educational opportunities or were to be born in a foreign country, many employers show little interest in actually changing the opportunities available to their employees when offering basic skills classes.

As Collins (1989) points out, the workplace literacy arena can be the site for power struggles between big business's desire to control the socialization and attitudes necessary to maintain a compliant workforce and workers' desires toward empowerment, decent wages, and safe work conditions. Auerbach (1990) examined excerpts from workers' ESL textbooks through the past hundred years and found that they presented a consistent philosophy of worker education: "that its purpose is to socialize learners into particular slots in the workplace hierarchy, teaching them to conform to employers' needs, accept the workplace as it is, and become 'good' workers" (pp. 223–224). Workplace educators may instead use the opportunity to help develop employees' abilities to speak up for themselves, to negotiate, to make suggestions, and to improve their working lives (Mawer, 1999).

THE POTENTIAL TO CREATE TRUE OPPORTUNITIES

Workplace literacy programs have numerous strengths. For employers, there are financial benefits as well as improved employee relations and increased productivity and quality. For society as a whole, there are great benefits to having a more literate citizenry. For workers, there are many conveniences that include participating in classes at their work sites and, in many cases, holding classes during paid work hours. This often gives adults with limited time, transportation, and childcare options the only practical way to attend classes. It is important that these benefits be combined with excellent instructional practices in order to help workplace literacy programs achieve their full potential.

Learner-centered literacy is not only able to meet learners' needs but also business needs. By encouraging workers to be-

come more instead of less, to speak out rather than being si-
lenced, and by using their creative energy and ideas rather that
suppressing them, learner-centered instruction embraces the
whole person as it encourages improvements throughout the
workplace.

Worker empowerment is not a goal embraced by all companies offering workplace literacy classes. For some, imparting
basic knowledge about filling out forms and understanding orders is all that is desired. However, for the many companies
committed to continuous quality improvement and team-based
organization, employee empowerment to make suggestions, solve
problems, take responsibility for their work, and implement
changes is essential. Many organizations today desire "Workers
who can learn and adapt quickly, think for themselves, take responsibility, make decisions and communicate what they need
and know" (Gee, Hull, & Lankshear, 1996, p. 19). In these types
of organizations, a curriculum built upon employees' needs and
concerns is the best way to involve workers in taking control of
their own learning and their own work (Schultz, 1992). Encouraging workers to write, speak, and read about topics and problems that impact their lives is a major step toward empowering
the participants to make positive changes in their work environment through their new communication skills.

Rather than using a deficit-based, teacher-centered model,
effective literacy programs foster learner autonomy and take action to change the communicative culture in the workplace.
This is achieved by creating incentives and opportunities for
learners and aiding them in developing a meaningful curriculum. The majority of language and literacy uses take place outside the classroom and workers must examine their learning experiences and develop their own communicative strategies as
they use language in the real world (Roberts et al., 1992). Dis-
solving the walls between the classroom and the work floor by
blending literacy learning and work problems makes the most
of the possibilities.

The issues and impact of workplace basic skills programs
remain contested areas of discussion. While there are great possibilities for workplace literacy, this potential is not always re-

alized. Now is the time for much needed changes to instructional techniques commonly used in workplace literacy programs. We cannot prepare workers for a continuously changing and technologically advanced workforce by using the old teaching techniques that have emphasized rote memorization, discrete skills, and assimilation into the existing work order. Instead, learning that emphasizes critical thinking, problem posing, and creativity is needed. By simply asking learners about their current literacy practices and goals, rather than assuming that their needs are identical to those of their employers or educational providers, and offering opportunities for them to name and change their world, worker educators can better serve their students.

CHAPTER 2

Expanding Definitions of Literacies and Learning

Literacy education is not only about learning to decode sounds and words. The way we learn to read and what we learn to read are also essential to successful literacy attainment. We must consider the affective and social needs of the learners and the reasons they want to learn in order to provide optimal education. This chapter looks at different approaches to defining and teaching literacy. How we are taught affects our attitudes and behavior and "when learning primarily entails a process of rote memorization, then learners develop attitudes of passivity and deference to external authority" (Canadian Labour Congress, 2001, p. 11). On the other hand, learning which is actively led by learners imparts values of confidence, initiative, and action.

Despite the need for a new type of worker who can think critically, solve problems, and take initiative, many workplace programs are still using old methods of training workers that inculcate outdated values. Even while workers are being taught innovative methods to solve the company's problems and empowered to make improvements, the classroom teaching methods send the contradictory message of "listen, follow directions, and don't ask questions" (Gee et al., 1996). By schooling workers in these archaic methods and values, organizations are missing the opportunity to tap into the knowledge and ideas of workers which are essential to success in the changing workplace.

Literacy which is empowering should be a goal of, not a threat to businesses. This type of workplace literacy serves both business and humanitarian purposes. It is beneficial to workers who learn to question, investigate, and become self-directed life-long learners, and to their organizations who benefit from these skills. If workers are not free to express their opinions, share their knowledge, or suggest improvements without fear, their enthusiasm and interest in the well-being of the organization are quickly lost.

When I took my first graduate class in adult education and heard about the political implications of literacy, I was puzzled. It did not seem that teaching people to sound out words was a terribly political act. I had been teaching workplace literacy for a few years and it appeared straightforward enough; both companies and workers would benefit greatly from literacy classes. But the more I thought, read, and observed, the more I found that the very limited skills offered and the way in which they were taught did not truly offer opportunity for workers to improve their circumstances. I saw that job classifications were divided not by reading skills, diligence, or capability but more often by race, gender, class, and ethnicity. Though teaching people to read is the basic purpose of literacy classes, how, why, and what they learn to read make a crucial difference in the outcomes. Paulo Freire's work has broadened the definition of literacy to include political understanding and cultural change because illiteracy is not just a learning problem, it is largely a socioeconomic and political issue. Freire argued that education cannot be neutral; it must either support or challenge the existing social system and that providing purely technical training in literacy and narrow job skills rather than critical thinking skills limits workers' opportunities (Freire, 1996; Freire & Macedo, 1987).

Educators who deny or are naïve about the political implications of literacy may actually contribute to educational inequities and may find themselves used as gatekeepers maintaining the subservience of the organization's workforce (Mawer, 1999). Whether the focus of a literacy program is to reinforce the organizational status quo or to create tools for improving workers' lives both inside and outside of the workplace is a question of utmost importance. Reading words written from a corporate perspective at face value and reading the world of work as we experience it can offer quite different meanings.

WHAT IS LEARNER-CENTERED LITERACY?

For workers, literacy education may be looked to as a means of creating greater mobility and security as globalization, new technology, and the resulting organizational downsizing and restructuring make workers increasingly vulnerable to job loss and change. Workplace literacy programs can help to empower working people by ensuring that they have the skills they need to negotiate and navigate the power structures at work. Instead of preparing employees to function more successfully in the existing social order, worker-centered education prepares them to transform social relations and shape their roles in the workplace (Auerbach, 1990). It helps them to find ways of making their voices heard and to realize that their opinions and communication styles are valuable. It encourages them to question, critically evaluate, and discuss issues and policies which impact their lives.

Rather than promoting a narrow and traditional approach to literacy in which the encoding and decoding of company forms is a central focus, worker-centered literacy goes further to improve conditions and safety, build relationships, and solve problems in the workplace. By creating opportunities for these relevant and meaningful learning experiences, workers may gain the confidence to ask questions, go to the personnel office and discuss work situations, and speak up about their opinions for improving the company. Finding their voices in this way allows learners to take more control and responsibility in their jobs. As one student explained the impact of the ESL program, "Before we were too scared to go to the office . . . now we know more English and we're not scared!"

The Canadian Labour Congress (2000) lists several key elements to worker-centered learning: it helps workers to have more control over their lives and jobs, it builds confidence and self-esteem, it builds on workers' strengths, it addresses the needs of the whole person, it involves workers in educational decision making, and it reflects the diverse learning styles and needs of adult workers. Learning by discussing ideas rather than memorizing facts, and by considering possibilities rather than accepting the status quo, are key tenets of learner-centered approaches to literacy. It respects, identifies, and builds upon the knowledge and skills workers already possess and incorporates topics and materials that they will actually use.

Rather than being dependent on the instructor, learner-centered literacy develops learner autonomy. Workers learn how to learn on their own, independent learning strategies are developed by practicing new study skills as well as by identifying and validating the strategies that workers are currently using. This approach recognizes that workers who are bilingual or bicultural have skill assets rather than liabilities and that different does not equal deficient (Elish-Piper, 2000). Learner-centered literacy is based on the notion that workers are the experts in their workplace, language, culture, and needs and have much to teach others. We remind learners that "No one knows everything and no one knows nothing" (Purcell-Gates & Waterman, 2000). Workers who have learned how to support a family on a minimum wage paycheck or who have left their homes to venture across hostile borders to find jobs in a country where they don't know the language are shown that these very characteristics of persistence, bravery, resourcefulness, and risk taking will also help them in learning to read.

A learner-centered approach views literacy as a social and cultural practice. It acknowledges that different types of literacy are needed depending upon context and that use of standard English is not the sole model for literacy (Gee et al., 1996). It allows that different people in different situations and cultures engage in very different literacies. These literacies may include choices about the language or dialect used in various situations and the collaboration of reading and writing with others. Levels of formality, style, degrees of directness, and politeness vary greatly depending upon social context. The language that learners use in their neighborhoods and with their coworkers may be very different from the kind they need at job interviews and for dealing with governmental officials. By acknowledging that learners' current literacy practices are legitimate rather than incorrect or nonexistent, the stage is set to expand their repertoire of literacy practices to include standard English in addition to their own cultural traditions. Rather than attempting to suppress or eradicate their current literacy practices, learners may instead look at how different language styles are used and by whom, in order to uncover the relationships between language, knowledge, and power (Demetrion, 2000).

Workplace literacy programs which are action-based and participatory are not as simple to set up and evaluate as more traditional programs, and the "messiness" of allowing learners' input into program design and content often discourages implementation of these methods. Because student-centered, participatory programs based upon learners' own agendas take control away from the teacher and employer in unpredictable ways, they have seldom been used in workplace literacy programs in the United States.

People are not merely workers, they are also physical, spiritual, and social beings whose aspirations are not limited to their roles on the job. Especially in areas of repetitious labor where there are limited opportunities for creativity, advancement, and interest inherent in the work itself, it is necessary for workers to find fulfillment outside of their job tasks. As Gowen (1992) found in her study of hospital workers, learners held little interest reading instructions for how to mop a floor and, not surprisingly, found it dull and demeaning. Likewise, factory workers find limited value in reading forms and regulations with which they are already too familiar. By embracing the multifaceted talents and energies of people, literacy education can be more helpful than focusing upon a narrow role, particularly when that role is deemed comparatively unimportant. Unlike professionals whose job status may positively reinforce their self-identity as a teacher, doctor, or executive, many workers see themselves first as family members and providers and much less significantly as machine operators or bus boys (Gallo, 2001).

By engaging learners through discussions of workplace concerns and personal experiences in a learner-centered curriculum, educators can begin to incorporate the reading, writing, and speaking skills important in workplace communication. A learner-centered curriculum is one that emerges from learners' interests and needs during the course of a program. Rather than focusing upon an imported and often irrelevant curriculum with predetermined content, the emphasis is on discussing learners' current needs and taking steps to meet them. Filling in blanks on a worksheet has limited interest or possibility for real-life application. However, writing a memo to the company president about an potentially dangerous situation which is then addressed and changed is a very tangible and real literacy practice. While general goals such as improving reading and writing skills may be set up in advance, learners' own needs will dictate the topics and activities that will fulfill these goals. Appealing to learners' interests and giving them skills that are immediately useful in their lives at work and beyond are key components of an "emergent curriculum," the development of activities that arise from learners' needs.

Embracing rather than ignoring workers' concerns is essential to a successful program. Following a strict lesson plan, "Today we are going to discuss Unit Three," when learners are visibly upset over an announcement that their bonuses have been cut or excited that laid off friends are being called back to work, ignores both the needs of the learners as people and the opportunity to engage them in a potentially transforming and practical learning experience. By talking to learners about their current concerns and introducing real-life materials: utility bills and notes from school as well as workplace forms, memos, and letters, the curriculum can become both flexible and relevant. We are able to introduce the technical vocabulary and mastery of work documents by involving the class in participatory activities. At the same time, workers are encouraged to create learning projects which are personally meaningful and lead to taking action to bring about positive changes in their work and lives.

In this way, learner-centered programs teach workers about grammar and spelling, phonics and pronunciation, but those skills do not become the center of their learning. They are the tools used to get at the heart of the issue. The techniques that workers learn toward more effective reading and writing are instruments used in the creation of a better life. The essential literacy is in reading the world with a sense of love, justice, and hope. It is learning both to speak up and to listen, to discern and tell the truth about our world, our work, and ourselves.

HOW IS LITERACY DEFINED?

The definitions of literacy have changed greatly over time (Kaestle, Damon-Moore, Stedman, Tinsley, & Trollinger, 1991) from being able to sign one's name, read the Bible, or vote to being able to interpret complex texts, analyze graphical information, and even use computers. The current trend is to define adult literacy in terms of employability and increased productivity. The 1988 amendment to the Adult Education Act defines workplace literacy services as "programs to improve workforce productivity by improving workers' literacy skills" (Askov & Aderman, 1991, p. 16). This definition implies that the highest goal is productivity and that literacy is merely a method toward achieving it. The Workforce Education Act, which provides most federal funding for literacy programs in the United States, is geared toward improving the literacy skills of the un- and underemployed in order to prepare them for the "technological workforce of the 21st century." This narrow definition of literacy puts the emphasis on the employers' needs for certain types of skills required in their companies rather than on learners' own needs and goals. By focusing solely on the role of learners as workers, rather than considering their other important roles such as parents, family members, citizens, community members, and consumers, a whole range of literacy purposes and possibilities is excluded.

This limited definition of literacy for workforce preparedness is also heavily biased toward measurable gains on standardized test scores and job placement statistics as the principal measures of learner and program success. Learners who want to improve their reading skills for other reasons such as helping their children with homework, becoming informed voters, studying religious texts, or increasing self-esteem and independence will not find their goals embraced by these employment-centered programs. Many workplace literacy programs in which training is provided on site-may have the even more narrow goals of teaching workers only to read specific company materials and to fill out company forms. This leads to "A common criticism of some workplace literacy programs . . . that they do not help workers become literate, rather they focus on job-specific skills that are not easily transferred to other contexts (Elish-Piper, 2002, p. 19)." One of the most common definitions of literacy focuses solely on the acquisition of technical skills in decoding text. It is supposed that learners who have obtained the skills of phonetic deciphering, syllabication, and finding the main idea in a paragraph will be equipped to apply these skills to successfully perform in any reading context. It implies a value-free toolbox which learners can bring with them to fix any literacy tasks they may encounter. Because the skills are easily measured and tested as well as familiar to most teachers, students, and employers, they provide a comfortable framework for planning, teaching, and evaluating workforce literacy programs.

A closely related concept of literacy is the idea of acquiring the ability to complete specific tasks or competencies such as filling out forms or following work instructions. Again, it is supposed that these learned competencies will then apply to a wide variety of literacy situations. However, as I have seen many times, the skill of reading in the atmosphere of a supportive and safe classroom versus reading out loud to a supervisor on the plant floor is akin to the experience of walking on a painted line on the floor compared to walking on an elevated high wire. The skills are ostensibly the same but the reality of the context changes the degree of difficulty.

It seems that in some circles the literacy wars have become unnecessarily divisive with battle lines drawn between phonics and whole language advocates or critical and functional literacy practitioners. Not many people will learn to read solely by memorizing phonetic sounds in isolation and just as few pick up great literary works and master them through sheer joy. A learner-centered curriculum can give balance with learners making important decisions about how and what they would like to learn. The educator's role is to show them options and offer opinions rather than forcing a favored methodology upon them. This allows learners to discover for themselves the techniques most effective for their own individual styles of learning.

Skills-based and competency-based notions of literacy are those most frequently found in workforce literacy programs (Hull, 1997a). Both focus on deficits in learners' knowledge and behavior rather than learners' strengths and capabilities. These approaches can be demoralizing and fail to use learners' current learning strategies and successes. The assumption is that literacy instruction is remedial and that learners need to be retaught things that they ought to have picked up earlier. These feelings are often internalized by the learners themselves, who may believe that they have failed within the educational system. Workers are often blamed for not taking advantage of educational opportunities when in fact they have been systemically excluded from participation. They are also blamed for their lack of skills and their inability to advance at work. In the workplace, people singled out as lacking the requisite literacy skills are often blamed for poor quality, inferior service, and the decline of the country's productivity as a whole (Hull, 1997b). Literacy becomes a political issue because it is both a contributor and result of inequity and poverty. The term *illiterate* has negative connotations, suggesting ineptitude, ignorance, and lack of cultural refinements. There is an attitude of condescension by society at large toward these so-called illiterates, ranging from pity to blame. In the United States where everyone is supposed to have equal access to quality public education, there is often a sentiment that those who have not learned to read have failed to use the opportunities given to them. This view exists despite overwhelming evidence that poor and "minority" students are not offered the same educational resources as their wealthier, white counterparts (Kozol, 1992).

Adults frequently build negative self-images based upon their past failures and it can be a challenge for workplace educators to help peel away their misconceptions about their own abilities and opportunities. By discussing our experiences critically, we may begin to realize that what we perceived as personal failings or shortcomings are shared by others and that larger societal and political forces rather than individual weaknesses are responsible for many of our life situations and academic successes or struggles.

Once when we were kidding around in class, I laughingly said to a man, "Don't be stupid!" and saw him immediately flinch and fall into silence. My careless words dredged up memories for him of shame and failure in another classroom. We often accept others' characterizations of who we are and what we can and cannot become. The scars caused by early educational experiences cannot be easily healed and must not be ignored by adult educators. Education should help people to recognize that they already have valuable knowledge and to invite people to believe in themselves (Freire, 1973/1993). It is important that educators do not permit our teachings to delimit people but expand their capabilities to fulfill their dreams. Learner-centered classes can help to impart a sense of pride in adults' achievements of learning to read or succeeding in a new country where their difficulties and victories are seldom acknowledged. Such programs may "educate students not only to make choices and to think critically but also to believe that they can make a difference in the world" (Giroux, 1992, p. 19).

The use of texts and materials that reinforce workers' subordination are one reason traditional workplace literacy programs are often viewed with skepticism by learners (Auerbach, 1990). A typical ESL textbook exercise which prescribes appropriate ways for workers to respond to supervisors' criticisms was mocked by my students who displayed exaggerated cowering and bowing motions as they read the script: "I'm sorry. Now I understand. I'll do it right this time." Such seemingly innocuous lessons can be viewed by working adults as offensive and belittling. Another common competency in the curricula of workplace literacy programs is reading the employee rulebook, hardly the sort of gripping, page-turning material that leads to a love of reading. Rote memorization and drilling of decontextualized vocabulary and grammar structures are also unlikely to result in the sophisticated fluency required within the cultural arena of the workplace. Exercises such as these that workers find demeaning do not provide the needed level of interest and involvement required for a truly engaging literacy program that impacts learners' lives.

Using language for real purposes engages both our hearts and minds, while trudging through endless readings selected only for their semantic simplicity dulls our thinking as well as our desire to learn. Even parrots learn profanities so readily not because these are the phrases most easily pronounced but because the animal senses that the strong emotion behind them is important and thus is retained. In the same way, it is more difficult for us to learn from nonsensical and boring materials such as "the cat sat on the mat" than to remember and use those which have true emotional impact, though their level of phonetic complexity may be higher. Words like "promotion," "discrimination," or "accident" begin to stir stronger emotions and lead to engaging discussions about workers' own experiences.

The enthusiasm generated by workers sharing their personal stories and images positively impacts the amount and quality of writing, reading, and discussion going on in the classes. In comparison to the sometimes lackluster responses generated from questions about textbook workplace scenarios and the usual company-related materials (memos, employee rulebook, production sheets), the opportunity to work with topics of their own choosing and creation has a powerful effect on the degree and type of participation in class. One manager also noticed that a learner-centered class had "changed the morale of the people, they feel that someone is interested in them as individuals and not just another body to do the work."

Historically, some employers have been concerned that educating workers excessively could incite them to demand better conditions, wages, and opportunities (Askov & Aderman, 1991). The type and amount of education that the working poor should be allowed are still contested areas today. Literacy is associated with power and the access to this power has many repercussions. In the United States there were at one time laws forbidding anyone from teaching slaves to read. Withholding literacy in this way ensured the subordination of illiterate groups. Today there still seem to be restrictions on the literacy skills allowed to the lower classes. Basic skills in decoding texts for the purposes of low-wage employment are all that are afforded to many of the poor people in our country.

For too many workers, deference to authority, compliance, obedience, and punctuality are the values stressed in their training, rather than creativity, leadership, and critical-thinking skills. The narrow training offered to workers in filling out forms and following directions is insufficient to help them advance and succeed in meaningful ways in an increasingly complex and technical age. By providing working-class learners equal and meaningful educational opportunities, employers may ensure that these workers are not left behind. Critical literacy raises awareness of the disparities in educational opportunities that are provided for different groups and seeks to eliminate these inequities.

The work of Paulo Freire was developed in the 1960s during a literacy campaign to teach Brazilian peasants to read. In *Pedagogy of the Oppressed* (Freire, 1973/1993) he advocated a method of learning through dialogue based upon the Christian principles of love, humility, hope, faith, and trust, in which the teacher and students explore problems together. Literacy by this definition is not only reading text but also critical reflection and transformative action, not merely reading words but also "reading the world." Freire's empowering and freeing approach to education encourages learners to create and express their own knowledge of the world.

Critical literacy challenges the existing social system, promotes change, and encourages creation of culture and knowledge. Learners consider problems in order to make changes in their lives and communities. The teacher's role is that of a problem-poser, asking questions and helping in the discovery of knowledge rather than of an expert problem-solver dispensing answers. The act of problem-posing involves listening, dialogue, and action. First the teacher listens to students' concerns, then these themes are presented in class in a different form such as a picture or story, and learners discuss them, ask for causes, and plan solutions. Finally, learners take action to bring their ideas outside the classroom.

Though critical, learner-centered, participatory approaches may be unfamiliar to many learners as well as educators, they are readily embraced as their effectiveness in engaging and helping workers to learn is realized. Emphasizing learners' own control over their education rather than the learned passivity and overreliance on an instructor turns the question of "What do you want me to write about?" into "What do *you* want to write about?" Learners who have acquired critical-thinking and decision-making skills are better off personally and have more to offer society and employers than those who have solely been given the opportunity to learn the narrow and momentary business-mandated job skills. Delimiting the possibilities and richness of literacy education to the constraints of mere job training is neither conscionable nor effective. When business interests focus on problem-solving learning programs rather than problem-posing ones, they limit the questions and the issues that can be raised by workers. Learner-centered approaches assure that the logic of the workplace in which profit takes precedence over humanity is not allowed to go unquestioned. The following chapters offer practical suggestions for implementing critical, learner-centered approaches in the workplace classroom. In this way we can better provide learners with "the skills they will need to define and shape, rather than simply serve, in the modern world" (Giroux, 1992, p. 18).

CHAPTER 3

Starting Up a Program

Getting a program started can seem like the most daunting part of the process. Even after everyone has come to agreement that it is a good idea to offer literacy classes, getting all the little pieces into place can be challenging. However, using a learner-centered rather than top-down approach offers flexibility and shared responsibility for planning and implementation. This is the time to explore possibilities, to be creative with available resources, and to generate enthusiasm. Getting started takes a just few basic steps. First, talk with everybody involved. Find out what workers' hopes, dreams, and expectations are for this program. Then recruit learners, set up the time and place, and begin classes. Remember that no program will ever be perfect, because it is an ongoing process; changing, fluctuating, and limitless. Allow some slack. Don't get too rigid with the structures and rules. Avail yourself of the many resources found on the World Wide Web, Educational Resources Information Center (ERIC), and local literacy providers, but be mindful of the underlying purposes and philosophies. Consider if they advocate learner-centered education and worker empowerment.

Some guidelines, steps, and ideas follow, an outline of considerations to get you started. You needn't follow them to a T since each organization has different needs and resources that can be customized according to their particular situation. There will be trials and errors, but if approached with good faith, dedication, and a sense of humor, wonderful learning can occur.

GARNERING SUPPORT AND
BALANCING DESIRES

Involving essential people in the program planning is key to successful implementation. Although the training department or upper management may be the impetus behind the literacy program, they are not the only, or even the most important parties to consult. Workers who will be participating in classes must be involved in the planning and decision-making early on. Programs in which learners are not allowed any input, but are just ordered to go to class are unlikely to be successful. Generating interest and enthusiasm for the program, finding creative ways of incorporating suggestions, and disarming naysayers are crucial during the planning phase. Short informational meetings with small groups are a good way to gain support through straightforward conversations that address the program plans and begin dialogues: What needs do you see in this organization? What learning opportunities would you like to have? Here are some possible classes that we can offer. Here's why. Here's what's in it for you. What are your suggestions and concerns?

Though worker unions are traditionally supportive of worker education, they may be opposed to literacy classes that are management-directed and feel that such classes will be used to discriminate against workers with lower test scores, regardless of seniority and job performance. The goals of unions and management for a literacy program may be quite different. Be sure that all groups are heard and represented in discussions. Some goals such as increased production will be primarily of interest to management while others such as being able to help kids with their homework will be goals of workers, but issues such as safety awareness, accident reduction, morale, and skill improvements are likely to be desired by all groups.

Make sure that supervisors understand and support the basic skill program instead of viewing it as a burden. The influence of immediate supervisors and coworkers upon the attendance and attitudes of employees in basic skills classes can impact the success of the program (Moore, 1999). Supervisors are frequently rewarded or punished for the quantity of the production output in their department. Taking workers off the job for several hours a week to attend reading classes makes their jobs much more difficult immediately with only a vague and far-off promise of improved productivity through increased literacy at some point in the future. Involved supervisors are encouraging, often stopping by the classroom to inquire about learning topics or to compliment workers on their improving skills.

Coworkers are more likely to be supportive if they are not required to increase their own workload while other people attend classes. Learners are sometimes subject to the pressures of making up the work they missed during class time and feeling indebted to or resented by coworkers who must fill in for them. Employees who are discouraged from leaving their work to go to class are unlikely to leave. In one company where I taught, the Latino workers reported being harassed by "the white guys" who blamed the ESL class participants for the company's decreased profit-sharing program because they were missing 4 hours of work per week by attending classes. Workers who are given the ostensible option of whether to attend classes and leave their coworkers to pick up the slack may well decline to attend and be further denigrated for their refusal to participate.

All levels of the organization need to understand and cooperate in order to make the program successful. Ask about communication throughout the organization. It is often surprising to find that the problem does not rest only with the workers presumed to be low-literate, but in the writing and speaking practices of better-educated employees as well. Emphasize that adjustments may need to be made by everyone, not only by the language minority and low-literate workers. A weakness of too many workplace literacy programs is the absence of follow-up in transferring learning from the training room to the job. Particularly for ESL students, newly acquired English-speaking skills may be more often met with impatience and criticism by supervisors than encouragement because the old ways of communicating through translators and hand gestures are easier to accommodate than the time-consuming decoding of new English in the busy workplace.

Identifying the needs to be addressed by literacy programs

is an ongoing and reflexive process. Basic skills programs are often begun in response to a problem. Find out what the perceived problem is. Are employees struggling with new procedures, paperwork, team structures, or technology? Is morale low? Do supervisors feel that current communication is inadequate? Is there a foreign language gap? Is most communication in spoken or written English now? How and why is this changing? How have these problems been addressed so far? Why have literacy classes been chosen to address these problems? Why now? Is literacy tied to a quality initiative? Can it be tied to a diversity, foreign language, or company-wide communication initiative? Who will benefit from this program and in what ways? How does this tie into the organization's mission statement? Are these literacy-related challenges or do they have more to do with discipline problems or overall organizational culture? What are barriers to participation? How will these be addressed?

IDENTIFYING NEEDS AND GOALS

An essential step is to identify the goals of the literacy initiative. Possible program goals include the following:

- Better organizational communication
- Less reliance on translators
- Improved morale
- Improved self-confidence
- Preparation for further training
- Improved participation at meetings
- Certification or citizenship achievement
- Increased employee retention and promotability
- Improved safety
- Enhanced quality, service, or productivity
- Benefit provided for workers' self-improvement

Ask learners about their personal goals and help them to identify specific areas that are important to them. Many learners have only a broad idea initially of wanting to write better or improve their reading skills, but these can be narrowed into more tangible goals that can be more readily measured. Being able to communicate more confidently with supervisors, to help children navigate the educational system, or to read bills and letters are common goals for learners. If the company is not clear about organizational goals, offer some suggestions, preferably ones that will be achievable and easy to document (see Chapter 7). Do we want to improve on-time delivery? Reduce accidents due to misunderstandings? Provide classes as a perk to reward workers? Be aware that there may be discrepancies between stated and actual program goals. There are spoken and unspoken expectations of programs that may not even be fully recognized until the expectations are unmet. Boyle (2001) suggests that though concerns such as competition may be given as the ostensible reason for program implementation, it might actually be used as a means of boosting employee morale or expressing humane organizational values.

Put goals in a simple mission statement in order to clarify and focus the goal. For example, "We would like all our service employees to read and understand the health benefits plan," or "All employees will read and write English well enough to fill out an accident form unassisted." Give concrete and specific goals if they need to be measured. Ask: How will we know that the program is successful?

It is important to be realistic with anticipated outcomes. Setting up your program and employees for failure by creating unrealistic expectations is harmful. Make sure that workers will not be expected to read college-level texts such as chemical labels, contracts, or operating instructions after only 40 hours of class. Boyle notes that many programs are characterized by "unrealistic expectations and inadequate investment" (2001, p. 7). Reasonable, incremental changes in reading levels and language proficiency are more likely to be produced than skyrocketing grade-level measurements and overnight organizational success.

Workplace literacy classes may be needed as preparation for more advanced training. Sometimes, it is not until the worker is struggling in computer or statistical process control training that the need for more basic skills is noticed. Then it is often too late. The worker has failed in one class and is stigmatized and discouraged by having to take a remedial course. Employees who will be changing job tasks or requiring additional training in the areas of job skills, communication, and technology may be better prepared by first completing basic skills training. Consider the following questions: What training is currently offered? Who is getting training opportunities now? Who is left out? Can basic skills bridge the gap to allow employees to take more difficult training?

Other important questions that require consideration are: How do workers see their roles? How do they perceive their skills and deficiencies? What have their previous educational experiences been like? How do they define success? How do they use text in and out of work? What do they want and expect from a program? Do workers want classes to include reading, writing, math, speaking, ESL, critical thinking, computer skills, problem solving, GED preparation, learning to learn, technical information, or work-related materials? Who will be invited to participate, everyone or only those singled out as "problem" people? Is the program viewed as punitive? By whom? Is it viewed as a reward? By whom? Will participation be volunteer or mandatory? Will workers be paid for all or part of their time?

Be aware that workers may not define success in the company or teacher's terms. Promotion and educational degrees may not be their goals. They may already feel that they are successful, that they have a good job, and assumptions otherwise are demeaning to them. The sense of community they have with their coworkers may be something they do not wish to jeopardize by being promoted to boss and becoming an outsider.

At one company where I taught, there were very different program goals perceived by management and workers. While management saw achieving English fluency as a key to job success and promotion, none of the production workers ever mentioned career advancement within the company as a goal. Workers realized the barriers they faced in education and language acquisition made the likelihood of significant job advancement unlikely. It also seemed obvious that all the supervisors in this company were men, and virtually all the people in higher positions were white Americans. Of the areas where English proficiency was needed in their lives, work was one of the least important for these immigrants. Because the jobs were allocated for non-English speakers, they were structured to require as little English communication as possible. For these workers, learning English was a way to help their children with school, to ask questions about their benefits and paychecks in the office, to communicate better with friends at work, and to interact in day-to-day situations in an English-speaking culture, rather than a key to advancement at work.

If funding is provided by a grant, the grant provider may have specific requirements such as assessing with a particular testing instrument or continuing with technical training. These requirements can be met along with the goals identified by program participants. According to the grant proposal for one literacy program, the purpose of these classes for the company included increasing employee promotability, reducing scrap, and improving on-the-job communication, particularly by reading and filling in forms. However, learners viewed the classes differently, as a tool for gaining power. They saw the program as an opportunity to learn how to navigate the educational system for their children, implement improvements at work, better understand work benefits, learn about computers, write checks, and gain greater freedom from relying on others to translate for them. By allowing learners to set the agenda for the skills and methods of learning in which they wish to engage, the class may become relevant and useful to their own needs and as well as to those of the employer and grant provider.

RECRUITING LEARNERS

Recruiting learners for basic skills classes is a sensitive process. Admitting to reading problems or limited English comprehension and taking the risk of making mistakes within the anonymity of a community college program is one thing. It is quite different to risk facing the scorn of coworkers and supervisors in the workplace where hard-won respect and politics are entangled with issues of competence and literacy.

Conducting a tour of the worksite can be a valuable tool for gaining an overall assessment of the organizational structures and needs. Be mindful that the person conducting the tour is likely to influence your perspectives. Plant workers pointing out dangerous conditions are very different than engineers showing off new technology. Observing workers on the job or getting to participate as a worker for the day can also be valuable experiences. Sitting in on meetings and training sessions will help you to get a feel for the type of spoken language that is used in these settings and who participates. Watching informal conversational activities during breaks and lunchtime can give an impression of the culture. Note if social groups are divided by gender, ethnicity, or language. These divisions are likely to be brought up by learners once classes begin.

People who need literacy classes the most may be unable to fill out an interest survey or read the memos announcing the classes. Small group discussions or one-on one interviews with an interpreter are often a better way of recruiting, soliciting input, and raising awareness about programs. At one company where I taught, hardly anyone checked off an interest in basic skills classes on a survey, despite a great need. However, once classes started, the information quickly spread by word of mouth and enthusiastic workers recruited their friends to come to class. The instructor can meet with small groups and let them know basic information about the class, discuss confidentiality, and answer questions. Merely meeting and talking with the instructor can reduce anxiety. Students are often reassured when the teacher is not the ogre they expected. Often fears and past negative educational experiences must be overcome. Many learners joke nervously on the first day of class wondering if I will be using a ruler or dunce cap to discipline them. Revealing the scars on their hands as well as the ones on their psyches is a reminder that past painful educational experiences are not easily forgotten.

The secret that is seldom revealed about workplace literacy is that done right, it is really, really *fun*. We laugh a lot and play and even sing sometimes, we poke fun at organizational hypocrisy fairly often, and we are able to share our true talents in storytelling, affirming, and teaching with one another. We begin to shed our timid and doubtful skins. Realizations set in as we ask the unaskable and think the implausible in considering new possibilities and examining current realities. We strengthen and soften as we learn new insights about ourselves and our fellow workers. We gain confidence in expressing ourselves, light bulbs ignite, and comprehensions click. We start to like this and we even start to get it, so we want to learn more. It's good and powerful stuff, and we need to convey that to potential learners.

CREATING INCENTIVES TO PARTICIPATE

People who already have more education are also more likely to participate in educational programs. They have often experienced success in educational settings and find it stimulating and even fun to participate in classes. The intrinsic motivations that very literate learners possess may not be apparent in low literate learners. People with less education are less likely to want to participate in classes; they may have had unsuccessful and even painful experiences with their past schooling. These learners may need incentives and encouragement in order to join in. Therefore, education that is directly linked to pay increases, promotions, or more desirable work is very popular. Consider what incentives can be provided for participating in and completing classes. Some companies offer gifts, celebrations, and recognition ceremonies for graduates. Others offer the chance to earn points toward purchasing goods at the company store, allowing spouses to take a class, field trips, or free vacation days. Ask workers what would entice them to take their first class and be creative. After the initial step is taken, it becomes easier to recruit learners to participate in additional courses.

COLLECTING EXAMPLES OF WRITTEN COMMUNICATION

Determining the skills needed in the workplace can be achieved in part by performing an audit based on worker's reports of their own literacy needs (see Figure 3.1).

Collect written materials to use during the planning and

Common Workplace Communicative Skills

What do people need to read at work?
Signs, manuals, forms, memos, instructions, newsletters, graphs, charts, maps, flow charts, blueprints, computer menus, labels, warnings, reports, letters, tickets, bulletin board postings.

What do they need to say?
Report problems, explain procedures, give suggestions, request assistance, speak at meetings, negotiate conditions, ask for directions.

What do they need to listen to?
Loudspeaker announcements, group meetings, one-on-one discussions, training videotapes, instructions, customer requests, telephone calls.

What do they need to write?
Notes, forms, e-mail, reports, evaluations, memos, suggestions, phone messages, letters, computer data entries.

Figure 3.1 Workplace Communication Skills

questioning process. Gather as many written artifacts as possible including those listed in Figure 3.1 as well as informal communication such as graffiti and handwritten notes. Find out how people feel about written communication now. Are there communications considered insulting or unnecessary? Are they poorly designed or written in an obtuse style? Are they legible? At one company, complaints were often made about workers filling out forms incorrectly. A sample form revealed a badly photocopied document in an eight-point font that I could barely read. If line graphs, pie charts, or tables are used frequently, it is important that they are also clear. Changing graph titles to a question such as "How many orders were delivered on time this month?" in conjunction with teaching graph reading facilitates understanding (DeFoe & Farrell, 2001). *Making it Clear* (Canadian Labour Congress, 1999) is a good source for learning how to improve the readability of documents through clear composition, use of appropriate graphics, and design. Offering clear language instruction benefits everyone in the organization, not just low-level readers, and avoids putting the burden of clear communication upon those with the least power and resources.

Many times the written communication that workers are exposed to is erroneous, illegible, or just nonsensical. At one company, a large scoreboard that perpetually read "Days without accidents: 417" was posted in front of the quality office even though there were several accidents each month. At another there were signs posted that read "Protective eyewear required in this area," but few of the employees wore safety glasses. The frequent disparity between written signage and reality makes workers suspect of the value of reading company texts (Gowen, 1992).

TESTING

If the program is funded by a grant, it is important to address grant requirements from program inception, and testing skills through standardized reading, math, and oral skills assessments is a common obligation. Will everyone take the assessment as a show of solidarity, or will problem people be singled out? It is not uncommon for supervisors and managers to be found lacking literacy skills when everyone is assessed. How will this be handled? Will they feel belittled taking a class with their supervisees?

In traditional programs it is a common practice to administer standardized reading and math assessments to all employees before beginning classes. However, some employees may suspect that the tests will be used to weed out low-scoring workers. Promises are usually made by the company management that the assessment results are confidential and only used to help people get the training they need. Mistrust of employer motives and promises is a foundational problem with many workplace basic skills programs (Milton, 1999; Rhoder & French, 1994). Promises such as, "this is not a test, this will not affect your job, these classes are provided to help you," offered by both management and educational providers throughout the literacy program process are usually met with suspicion by workers. Despite these disclaimers, many employees feel that it is naïve to believe that test results will not impact their on-the-job treatment. Workers up for promotions would likely be viewed less favorably once a basic skills training recommendation is known by management. Snickers are heard throughout the plant about the employees who "failed" the assessment and resentment is fostered in those who must now take classes. Refusal to participate in classes may result in termination whether or not that is the stated reason. Repeated assurances to the contrary only lead to greater skepticism and distrust of the programs. Low-literate workers may have especially high anxiety levels about test taking because of previous academic failure. Great consideration should be given to making this process as comfortable and confidential as possible if it must be done.

ELIMINATING BARRIERS IN THE ORGANIZATIONAL CULTURE

While some organizations may boast of their workforce literacy programs, viewing them as an opportunity for public relations and a valuable perk for employees, others are uneasy about calling attention to their low-skilled or immigrant workforce. Employees may also take their attitudinal cue from the way programs are presented. Companies that emphasize the confidential and private nature of their basic skills programs can give an air of shame and secrecy to the program that causes avoidance, while companies who publicly congratulate and reward employees who graduate call positive attention to the programs.

Even though organizations may encourage learners to attend classes, exclusionary communicative practices in a company culture which tolerates impatience, rudeness, and failure to accommodate beginning language learners' abilities are discouragements to using new literacy skills. Rapid, idiomatic speech in a noisy manufacturing plant is difficult to understand, even for native speakers of English, and for second-language learners, the situation is especially problematic. Additionally, because many Americans have never learned a second language, they are unaware of the difficulty of doing so and may lack the empathy for new language learners that is more common in other cultures. As Mawer (1999) has suggested, it is important to contextualize and understand the role of communicative practices throughout the workplace rather than designating learners as deficient and lacking in communication skills. The efforts made by native English-speaking employees to slow down and simplify their speech, as well as to become better listeners and clear writers are a great help to basic skills learners.

Identify problem areas, expectations, and possibilities of noncompliance that are not literacy related. Are the workers mad about something? Are there disincentives to displaying literate behaviors? Are they getting mixed messages? Not all work problems are literacy problems. Failure to fill out forms correctly can also be a result of resistance, overwork, or anticipated punishment (Defoe, Belfiore, Folinsbee, Hunter, & Jackson, 2001).

In some cases, workers are even punished for *correctly* filling out documents such as accident reports, scrap sheets, or statistical process control charts. Workers may find that their honesty and diligence in completing paperwork accurately lead to reprimands or financial punishments. In one case a worker related that after filling out his scrap sheet correctly for a year he was told by his supervisor that they could not give him a standard pay raise because he had produced too much scrap. The next year he deliberately filled out his reports inaccurately and was monetarily rewarded for decreasing his scrap production by such a substantial amount. Workers in such situations quickly learn to become "incompetent" in these areas of literacy.

Most of us try to read the world before we read the words. I have a number of computer software manuals stacked dusty and unused under my desk, although reading the manual may be the "right" way to learn an application, many of us find it more useful to play around with the program or ask someone to show us how to use it before actually cracking open the book as a last resort. One woman told me, "Everyone I know would have to be dead before I opened a manual." I don't always fill out my work forms correctly, not because I lack the literacy skills to do so, but because I am in a hurry and do not give it my full attention. Expecting people to be excessively text dependent, regardless of their literacy levels, is unrealistic.

ESTABLISHING THE ROLE OF THE WORKPLACE EDUCATOR

Mawer aptly describes adult educators as being "in the workplace but not of it" (p. 112, 1999). This liminal role is valuable as it affords educators the unique chance to see the workplace culture in ways that are often opaque to those belonging wholly inside or outside of it. By being in the workplace, adult educators can take on a positive role as a liaison between workers and management, advocating for workers as well as bringing about change. As outsiders, they have a unique perspective on the complex culture of the workplace which can be brought to light by discussions with those inside the culture. Such discourse has the potential to bring about significant changes in attitudes and practices at work where "business as usual" is rarely questioned.

Folinsbee (2000) suggests that workplace educators must be flexible, creative in developing learning materials from available resources, and politically astute. Good workplace practitioners are also skilled in advocacy, analysis, intercultural communication abilities, and the specific instructional skills needed for adults in the workplace. By setting up a partnership with an educational provider that has expertise in adult learning and literacy, organizations can benefit from these skills. Many companies partner with universities, community colleges, or other literacy experts as their educational providers. These organizations often have experience in writing and securing grants to pay for the classes. As well, they possess instructional expertise and offer an added measure of confidentiality.

It is a mistake to think that anyone can teach English just because that person speaks it, or that anyone can teach reading just because that person can read. The techniques used with children and with other training programs are not always suitable or effective for adult literacy classes. It is important that educators are sensitive to the dynamics of the workplace in which learners may have little choice about their own participation in training. The power structures of workplace learning are very different from those of programs in which learners enroll voluntarily and can leave at will. Seemingly innocuous classroom requests may be viewed as coercive or threatening by worker-learners.

While many programs rely heavily on volunteer tutors, they can easily become discouraged or quit, leaving their tutees in the lurch. Issues of comfort and confidentiality are also important to consider with tutors. While tutors may be well-meaning and enthusiastic, they seldom acquire enough expertise during a few hours of tutor training to be able to deal with the complexities of adult reading difficulties or second language instruction. Supplementing professional instructors with tutors can be an option, and training former basic skill students to be peer-tutors is positive way of mentoring. Peer mentors are valuable because learners can see people like themselves who have succeeded in improving their literacy. Mentors of different backgrounds are valuable in helping to build relations and understanding across the borders of class, race, and language.

Understandably, most businesses have not given much thought to literacy. Some may assume that everyone can read, write, and understand verbal communication well. Others may not believe that it is possible for their workers to improve their skills. One manager told a colleague of mine that he did not believe in offering ESL classes because: "I have a college education and I can't learn Spanish. How are *those people* going to learn another language?" Workplace educators have the important and sometimes exhausting job of educating management about the potential and needs of "those people." It is essential that employers are informed about key issues in literacy. It is up to the educator to point out how long it takes to master a foreign language, how difficult it is for the average worker to read college-level chemical information, and how literacy limitations do not always translate to worker incompetence.

Make sure that literacy skills are not viewed as a magic decoder ring bestowed upon grateful learners by a benevolent organization but rather a mutual benefit and shared learning process. New reading or language skills are awkward at first; like a right hander using a left hand it is uncomfortable and unnatural to communicate in unfamiliar ways. A further barrier sometimes encountered is workers' lack of literacy in their first language. Many companies translate all of their documents into Spanish only to find that some workers are not able to read in their first language. Understanding the special needs of those not literate in their first language and their difficulties in learning to read in another language must be conveyed to employers. Creating awareness of these issues and finding ways of bridging the gaps between learners' needs and their work environments are key responsibilities for adult educators in the workplace.

SETTING UP THE FRAMEWORK

Answering the essential questions of how the program will be structured and who will be involved provides an armature for creating the rest of the program with the flexibility to meet learners' needs. Obtaining the input from a variety of voices within the organization about these key issues also provides opportunities for educating a cross-section of individuals about the program and its purposes.

Who Will Be Included in the Program?

A number of important questions must be addressed about who will be included in a literacy program: Which employees will be included? Is this part of a company-wide training program or are only those seen as deficient being singled out? Will workers be paid for their time in class? Who will do the peoples' jobs while they are in class? Will participation be voluntary? Will those with the greatest need or the first to sign up be given priority? Will there be childcare provided if it is after shift? Can children and spouses attend classes? In the first classes it is helpful to include employees who are likely to succeed, rather than starting with the lowest skilled or problem employees. This helps to ensure that the program will start off smoothly.

Another consideration is how to group classes by learning needs. Once I taught at a factory which put 3 African-American women into a class with 10 Indian women who spoke little English. When they saw the beginning level ESL textbook that started with learning the letters of the alphabet, the African-American women became rightfully angry, "Why are we doing this kindergarten stuff?" they asked. It is important to make sure that learners are grouped appropriately. In many workplace programs, students are placed together for the convenience of production schedules rather than learners' needs. This can result in multilevel, multilingual classes where native speakers of English with reading difficulties are placed alongside immigrants with limited English proficiency. These very different literacy needs cannot be met by the usual instructional approaches and must be approached with care and creativity.

What Will Be Included in the Curriculum?

"Basic Skills," "Literacy," and "Reading" are course labels that can feel demeaning to some learners. "Communication Skills," "Business Writing," or "Essential Skills" can be better names that don't have connotations of deficiency. Signing up for a class should be a positive experience for workers, not an admission of guilt. Even saying "learners" rather than "students" or "trainees" suggests a self-directed approach to education that continues beyond the classroom rather than a teacher-dependent role. Learner confidence and esteem can be built up by dispelling the notions that nonstandard ways of communication are inferior and that limited literacy is an individual failing rather than societal problem.

Find out what and how workers would like to learn. What will be taught, life skills or employment skills? In a learner-centered classroom, it is not necessary to determine the curriculum ahead of time, it emerges during the course through workers' discussions and activities. However, for purposes of explaining the program offerings to potential participants, it is valuable to define general areas of learning.

Learning computer skills may have a status that makes it more desirable than learning literacy skills alone. At a company where we offer both basic skills and computer courses, only a couple of workers indicated interest in a basic skills class but dozens and dozens signed up for computer classes, including many who were unable to read even the basic menu commands. Basic skills combined with computer skills is a possible approach if computer access is available. If there is interest, it is easy and fun to incorporate basic computer skills into the literacy curriculum by creating a class web page, typing or editing learners' own stories, writing memos, and creating newsletters. Workers often boast that they are taking a computer class rather than just learning to read and write. However, computers may also provoke anxiety, especially for older workers. Some companies invest large amounts of money in self-study basic skill software programs that are never used because most people with limited language and literacy skills are uncomfortable using computers alone. Additionally, the confidence and self-directedness needed for independent computer study are rarely found in beginning literacy students. These attributes can be built and encouraged with support, but the majority of adults prefer a human teacher at least for their initial computer learning.

Learning how to learn brush up skills can be valuable for adults who have been away from formal education for a long time. These can include basic study skills in how to use a dictionary, do research in the library and on-line, take notes, use mnemonic devices for enhancing memory, practice and apply new knowledge, and create self-directed learning projects.

Other classes that should be considered as offerings in conjunction with basic skills include foreign language, cultural diversity, and clear English classes. First language literacy is also greatly needed but seldom provided in workplace programs. When I teach Spanish language classes for U.S.-born employees, I am often approached by Spanish-speaking workers who want to join as well in order to learn how to read and write their own first language. Providing a variety of courses through all levels of the organization reinforces the idea that communication is a shared responsibility, and that workers of all cultures and language backgrounds are equally valued.

Where Will the Classes Be Held?

Instructional space reflects the amount of value the company places on its classes and the physical setup of the classroom says a lot about the importance of the class and the learners. At some companies, the literacy classes are bumped into a noisy corner of the lunchroom whenever a couple of VIPs need the conference room. This sends the message that the learners and their program are of little value. I have also taught at companies where classes were held in a utility closet, a tiny trailer, or a filthy room filled with dead rodents. This shows little respect for the workers or their learning needs.

A dedicated space where learners can feel comfortable and call their own is important. Ideally, quiet and well-lit rooms with a whiteboard or a flip chart, chairs and tables should be provided. I prefer a flip chart to a whiteboard because I can take the pages with me to type up the stories and brainstorm ideas that learners have generated in class. The company should also provide pencils, erasers, dictionaries, notebook paper, and three-ring binders to hold learners' work and handouts. Providing quality materials including note cards and envelopes for learners to write real thank you notes, personalized printed stationery for correspondence, or colored pens and graph paper to create charts adds another dimension of value and authenticity to their writing that may not be found by scribbling in workbooks.

Privacy is also important. In one company we held classes

in the cafeteria while coworkers peered in the windows making faces and shouting "*burros*" (dummies) at the learners within. Arranging chairs into a circle facilitates a sense of equality and participation because it allows all participants to make eye contact and converse more easily than rows of students looking at each other's backs. It also puts the instructor on equal footing as a co-learner rather than the all-knowing authority. Small class sizes of less than 10 or 12 students are needed to allow everyone an opportunity to participate. Larger groups are more difficult to engage in discussions and do not get the benefits of necessary individualized attention.

Workers who are standing and doing physical labor all day are often noticeably sore and tired by the end of their shifts and the beginning of the class. Try to accommodate them by providing opportunities for them to move around. Make the room temperature as comfortable as possible. I have taught in plastic molding plants where the factory temperatures exceed 100 degrees, and spending class time sitting in the air-conditioned conference room was a welcome respite for these workers. Other times I have been in food processing plants where employees worked in freezers all day and sometimes reported feeling ill in the unaccustomed warmth of a heated office.

Make the class welcoming by providing or at least allowing food and drink. Coffee and donuts can make the atmosphere more casual and even a bit celebratory as sharing food does wonders to break down social barriers and dispel awkwardness. In some classes learners even take turns bringing in food to share their favorite recipes. Set up a resource center lending library where learners can check out books, software, bilingual newspapers, magazines, audiotapes, and videotapes relevant to their interests. Encourage workers to use these materials and to bring in their own materials to share with the class.

When Should Classes Be Scheduled?

Offering classes on paid time during regular working hours is the best option for most workers. Transportation, childcare, and other family obligations as well as second jobs make it difficult for many workers to participate in programs off work hours. While white-collar workers typically receive training during their normal schedule, production employees frequently cannot leave their work and are required to attend classes off shift. When on shift classes are not possible, companies may offer classes for two paid hours before or after workers' regular shifts 2 or 3 days per week. At one company where I taught, some of the students who worked the midnight shift voluntarily attended class in the early afternoon during their normal sleeping hours. While this demonstrates the dedication to learning found in many workers, such sacrifices should not be required.

How Long Should the Classes Last?

As with any language learning program, increasing the amounts of practice learners have improves their abilities. Literacy, like most unused skills, can atrophy quickly. Workers may lose the literacy skill they once had by many years of working in jobs where these skills are not exercised and also may lose some of their language skills during breaks of several months without classes. On the other hand, periodic breaks of a week or two between class terms can impart a sense of accomplishment and anticipation as one session is completed and the new classes are set to begin.

Meeting at least two to three times per week for several months allows workers to attain some noticeable skill improvements and determine how much more they would like to improve. Unfortunately, most workplace literacy classes meet less than 5 hours a week, which is insufficient to make serious progress in language skills. Classes that only meet once a week spend such a large amount of time reviewing the previous week's forgotten lessons that little is accomplished. The average 40–60 hour class without structures that encourage learner autonomy will not make a significant difference in most measurements of learners' skills. Ideally an ongoing program will continue for a year or more. However, by including learning how to learn strategies, changing organizational culture, and building safe communities of clear language usage, even a short program can begin to make a difference.

Once the basic structure has been sketched out and classes are planned and scheduled, the true fun can begin. The next chapter describes ways of incorporating literacy learning with real-life workplace problems in order to make the most of a workplace program for employees and employers alike.

CHAPTER 4

Engaging Literacy with Workplace Improvement Projects

By using learner-generated improvement projects, a range of issues may be addressed regarding concerns such as safety and miscommunication that engages learners and allows them to expand their literacy skills in real-life situations. Improvement projects are actions taken about issues that workers have identified as problematic at work. These may be as simple as noticing a dirty lunchroom and creating a sign that reminds people to pick up their trash or as complex as ongoing letter-writing campaigns, organization, and actions to bring about greater organizational change. The basic principle is that using language for real purposes is a better way of learning than using it for artificial classroom exercises (Krashen & Terrell, 1983). Improvement projects provide opportunities for workers to immerse themselves in language activities that both accelerate and enhance their literacy learning. Instructors who ask authentic questions in which the answer is unknown such as "What is the best part of your job?" and "What do you want to change about your workplace?" elicit genuine dialogue which is more meaningful than asking artificial classroom questions where the teacher already knows the answer such as "What color is this pen?" "What is the past tense of 'bring'?" or "How do you spell 'communicate'?" Knowing how to spell communicate is less important for adult workers than actually doing it.

Workplace improvement projects engage learners because they are real and something the workers care about. These projects may also produce concrete results and changes that positively impact workers' lives. My own students have seen that writing a memo to management about a broken microwave in the lunchroom can result in a new microwave, writing a safety suggestion can result in a $50 bonus and avoidance of accidents, and making a well-rehearsed phone call to the doctor's office can result in moving up an appointment date. The desired effects do not always come about, but there are more changes than learners get by conjugating verbs on a quiz. Even when they do not produce immediate results the small ripples created by learners' efforts are more far reaching both in the cumulative awareness they may bring to the outside world and the internal confidence that comes with the experiences. It encourages the people who sometimes feel they are forgotten or unimportant to speak up and to take actions which can make things happen.

EXAMINING AND IMPROVING
COMMUNICATIVE PRACTICES AT WORK

Although communication is generally defined as a two-way process, the larger burden of communicating at work is usually placed on the literacy learners whose attempts to use their new language skills are often met with impatience or rudeness by their coworkers. Workers sometimes express the sentiment that their opinions are not valued because they are immigrants or people of color. One man reported, "Because I don't speak English they don't believe me. Believe supervisor." Other workers relate that they have never received a compliment or thank you from their boss. Work can be a source of boredom, frustration, and daily humiliation as well as a means to build social support and personal pride. It is important to acknowledge all facets of workplace communication in literacy classes. Getting past workplace segregation to have real dialogues, if not as equals (this is, after all, work and hierarchies run deep) then at least as fellow humans instead of their stereotypical work roles, is a step in the right direction.

In *Seeds for Change*, workplace instructors are challenged "to venture beyond the confines of the class" (Canadian Labour Congress, 2001, p. 26) by engaging in an emergent curriculum that leaves behind certainties and engages possibilities. Initially learners may resist the new and unfamiliar learner-centered participatory approach to literacy and feel more comfortable with a traditional, teacher-centered, "fill in the blanks" dispensing of knowledge. Recently, during break I wrote up a list of discussion questions based on the current conversation we were having in class. When I passed it out, a student said to me in a surprised and almost accusatory tone, "You just made that up!" Though I was proud of my attempts to guide writing assignments around learners' immediate interests, some clearly saw this as an unorthodox and possibly unethical approach to teaching. It is important to explain why you are doing things in class so that nontraditional learning activities such as improvement projects, spontaneous curriculum, or sitting in a circle are not just viewed as disorganized, or disrespectful in comparison to learners' expectations from previous schooling (Rosow, 1995).

Find out how and where learners are currently using their literacy skills. Begin by asking questions such as where do you speak English now? Who speaks English to you? What do you need to read and write? In many workplaces there are few daily opportunities to use English or reading skills. One manufacturing engineer related that he communicated to workers largely through drawings, sign language, and showing examples of good and bad parts. Since the nature of their work was very concrete and errors were usually visible, it was easy to find ways of demonstrating and illustrating the correct work procedures. The noisy conditions of the plant also made gesturing preferable to shouting communications. A good way to start talking about on-the-job communication is to have learners bring in the tools or forms they use at work and explain their uses to the class. Go out into the work area and have workers guide you on a tour of their workplace to personally view their sources of job pride and frustration. As an outsider, the instructor may be unfamiliar with the jargon and technical vocabulary of the worksite. This is a great opportunity to work together as co-learners. Students may know the names of equipment and procedures and the instructor may know how to write them or the instructor may know some words for certain tools, but the workers know how to use them. Piecing together information in this way to create work specific vocabulary lists or dictionaries is a valuable and practical activity.

Organizational Integration

When coworkers in one area all speak the same foreign language there is seldom an opportunity to use English during their conversations. Roberts, Davies, & Jupp (1992) found that adult English learners have very little opportunity to use their new language skills because they are usually segregated in undesirable work areas with other immigrants. Their occasional contacts with native speakers are too often stressful interactions involving disputes with individuals perceived as having much greater status. They have few opportunities for the kind of unstressed conversation with peers in which language socialization and learning are most readily fostered. One of my students expressed the desire to have more opportunities to "catch English," a fitting metaphor for the contagious nature of language exposure. In many companies, even social events meant to improve employee relations are segregated by race, language background, class, or gender. Though the American staff members may participate on the bowling teams and in golf outings, the immigrants from the company often do not. "No time, no English," one ESL student explained. "Cost too much," another added. Find if it is possible to reduce segregation by language groups by allowing workers to move to different areas, encouraging mixed groups and participation in conversations with English speakers. This may not be comfortable for anyone at first, but such efforts greatly improve the communicative practices of the organization. As one manager noticed about ESL class participants "The more confident they feel, the more they attempt English—the more English they use, the better they get."

A U.S.-born worker complained angrily to me each day after the ESL class was dismissed, "You know, they just go back to speaking Spanish as soon as they leave this room!" This phenomenon of people preferring to speak in their own language and the antagonism felt by their English-speaking coworkers is common. It is important that first languages be respected throughout the organization and that learning English is seen as a added skill, not a means of eradicating first language use. Goldstein (1997) found that there were disincentives for immigrant production workers to speak English in their workplace, and that doing so separated them from the solidarity of their community. It is important to recognize that prestige, benefits, authority, and opportunities for advancement can come not only from speaking the dominant official language but also the unofficial minority language.

One creative way of fostering intercultural or even interdepartmental communication is to pair learners with a pen friend with whom they may correspond regularly. This can be done in English or in multiple languages and it challenges learners to improve their reading and writing skills while enhancing workplace communication. At some companies I have conducted a bilingual writing project involving a workplace English as a second language program for Latino immigrants working in a factory in conjunction with a Spanish language program for English-speaking coworkers in the same company. Learners from both groups experienced the difficulties in crossing boundaries of culture, language, and class at work as they learned to communicate in one another's language by exchanging letters.

When I asked my Latino ESL students what I should teach their Anglo coworkers in the Spanish class the most popular response was, "Tell them not to scream at us." This gave a good indication of the atmosphere of disrespect and poor communication found in the organization at the start of this project. In an attempt to foster improved relations, each ESL program participant was assigned a writing partner from the Spanish class and each partner sent the other a weekly letter written in the writer's first language. By exchanging letters with their pen friends, the Mexican workers were able to voice their concerns in their own language and build relationships that crossed the boundaries of status, race, and culture. They were also in the role of being the authority and helping the others learn Spanish as mentors.

I believe that teaching Spanish to American coworkers is beneficial for many reasons: it fosters empathy as they experience the true difficulty of learning a new language as an adult, it demonstrates to their Latino coworkers that their language and culture are valued, it helps them to gain the skills of rewording, repeating, slowing down and using nonverbal gestures in their conversations, and perhaps most importantly it allows them to interact on a personal level as fellow humans and co-learners with their employees rather than limiting their relations to giving orders.

Creating opportunities for these groups to communicate in nontraditional ways as co-learners of one another's languages was a small step toward eliminating some of these barriers within their work world. By getting to know their workers through corresponding and asking for help in translating their letters, those who engaged in conversations with the immigrants began to view them as fellow workers with their own personalities and feelings. Office workers began to comment on the immigrants' progress in English and to offer words of encouragement more frequently. Some English learners found allies in these Americans who took the time to listen through the heavy accents and imperfect grammar to discover the concerns of their fellow workers and offered encouragement to one another as they explored new communication practices. The Latinos from the factory also became more confident and capable about expressing their concerns to management. Writing in their first language gave these workers an opportunity to express themselves in ways that they could not do adequately in English. It also gave them a chance to improve their first language literacy.

As a result of increased communication between English and Spanish speakers during this learning project, there were some improvements and concessions in the efforts made by the native English-speaking employees to slow down and simplify their speech as well as to become better listeners. The Latino students also began to cross the boundary of being creators of written documents such as personal letters, life histories, and memos to management rather that merely being the recipients of written information. By experiencing first hand the difficulties of learning a foreign language, coworkers are able to have a better understanding of the hardships faced by the immigrant laborers studying English. Additionally, putting a name and face on the workers and building personal relationships can improve work relationships and encourage coworkers to rethink their own communicative styles. Crossing the line of trying to communicate with fellow workers from different culture, language, and class backgrounds as equals is a difficult and ongoing process that may be fostered by communicative programs such as this.

Encouraging Workers to Speak Up

One of the first barriers that workers need to overcome in literacy classes is the misconception that they are only the recipients of other people's texts, that reading is a one-way street, or that learning to decode the sentences, summarize the paragraphs, and check the appropriate boxes handed down to them is the extent of being literate. It is not. From the first minute of class, the instructor can begin writing down what workers say in their own words on the board, acting as a scribe to make their speech visible. Encourage workers to start writing; even if they are wary and say they can't write they can begin to copy the words they have spoken. Help them to realize that not only do they have something to say, but that it is something worthwhile that may be solidified in print and even distributed for others to read. One useful exercise is to have workers come up with a list of communication tips for English-speaking coworkers to use with new readers and English learners. These can include ideas such as the following.

Tips for Better Communication at Work

- Write clearly and simply.
- Don't shout!
- Rephrase, repeat.

- Slow down.
- Show, point, gesture, demonstrate, give an example, or draw a picture.
- Avoid idioms such as "in the ballpark" or "when pigs fly."
- Speak clearly and face the person you are talking to.
- Go to a quiet area to speak if possible.
- Listen.
- Be patient.

Encourage learners to brainstorm for ideas that would be helpful in their particular workplace. Creating such a list validates their knowledge about communicative practices and demonstrates the idea that communication is a cooperative operation, not a one-sided endeavor. Having learners present their tips to a group of supervisors at a meeting or performing a humorous skit showing do's and don'ts can be other ways of getting their message across.

Another good practice is to give supervisors lists of vocabulary that learners are working on. "Please turn off the machine," "Shut it down," and "Stop it" may all have the same intended meaning but are written and pronounced as three very different phrases. Getting coworkers to be consistent in using the same terminology simplifies the learning process and cuts down on misunderstandings.

Learning ways of using language in order to gain entrance to the domains defended by institutional gatekeepers is a valuable literacy skill (Cushman, 1999). "Put it in writing" joins "We are only discussing items on the agenda" as common dismissals of the concerns of workers made by those in power. Limiting access to discussion of workplace issues by invoking rules of "proper" language usage is a common way of silencing those who are not well versed in the discourse styles of the dominant group. Workplace literacy programs need to be able to help learners to use the preferred language and customs of workplace discourse for their own purposes.

Often, because people are reluctant and embarrassed to convey that they don't understand what they have read or heard, their coworkers are unaware of the problem. Too often supervisors feel that their messages have been adequately sent and understood without checking for comprehension. Once, after an English-speaking Human Resources manager had made an important presentation about workers' new insurance options, I asked the immigrants who had been in attendance if they had understood everything during the meeting. "No. Julie talk and Julie hear and I sit," replied one worker with dismay. "Did you ask any questions?" I inquired. "No." It seemed that often the communication gap was so wide that no questions could begin to bridge it. It is important to encourage supervisors and coworkers to ask questions to check comprehension using who, what, where, when, why, and how questions, not just "Do you understand?" A smile and nod may convey respect, hide embarrassment, or acknowledge the speaker, not necessarily indicate complete comprehension. As coworkers begin to encourage questions, learners may become more comfortable asking for clarifications. Learners may find that even if it is embarrassing to ask for repetitions or definitions that most speakers want to be understood and will clarify their thoughts, though they may need to be prompted and reminded regularly.

CRITICALLY READING WORKPLACE TEXTS

Just as there must be concessions and bilateral communication efforts in spoken interactions, so must organizations modify their written texts to make them more reliable and accessible for the current reading levels of the workforce. Even when beginning English students have a grasp of enough vocabulary and grammar to comprehend simple, straightforward statements, the subtleties of sarcasm, hidden agendas, and implications inherent in normal workplace conversation and writing are often lost on them. This is not naiveté on the part of the language learners, who are probably accustomed to duplicitous and insincere messages in their own language, but rather a lack of familiarity with the manner in which these messages are disguised in English. This problem is especially significant in a workplace setting, where official communications such as memos, announcements, and company policies may not be completely comprehensible, sincere, or straightforward. It is important to discuss these elements so students realize that not everything (especially corporate communications) can be taken at face value. Workplace literacy programs which teach workers to read words without reading between the lines are omitting one of the most important dimensions in workplace communications.

Gowen suggests employees may be resistant to obeying workplace texts in part because "They believe that only a person with no common sense, a person who is docile and easily manipulated would accept everything that is written down" (1992, p. 100). One common communication problem encountered at many workplaces is that there are often differences between what is written and what is actually done in the organization. For example, at one factory, the written policy stated that eating and drinking were not allowed in the production area. However, discrepancies between the written policy and actual practices were obvious to workers. Some supervisors did in fact allow eating and drinking in the production areas, just as some allowed them to work without safety glasses, contrary to posted signs. Learners also pointed out major discrepancies between the company's written safety policy and everyday practices: "Sometimes the alarms go off, they tell us to keep working," one student remarked. Such practices give further credence to workers' beliefs that written documentation is of little value. In contrast, the "real," unwritten procedures are quickly learned through observation and first-language conversations.

Realizing that "the reason I have trouble reading this is because it is badly written, nonsensical or just untrue," rather than "I can't read this because I'm not smart" is a big step. A fun exercise is to have employees write the "real" story—comparing what a text says with what actually happens. Another activity to consider is writing a guide for new employees. What is important for workers to know about this organization? What do learners wish they had known when they started here? What inside tips can they offer to newcomers through their own experiences and expertise?

Dissecting Workplace Documents

The ability to understand not only what you are being told but also why they are telling it to you is key to comprehension (Ehrig, 2001). Traditional workplace literacy instruction may merely take company documents at face value and use them to check reading comprehension and form-filling abilities. The excerpt from a company mission statement such as "Our customers are our top priority" might be tested as "What is our company's top priority?" With the only correct answer being "our customers." Instead, a critical reading of the text might ask learners to offer their own interpretations of writings. "The company manual says customers are our top priority, do you agree? Why?" or "This candidate for union representative promises to improve our working conditions. What do you think?" Or offer learners the chance to fill in the blanks with their own opinions: "This company's top priority is _____." The idea that a text might be true from one person's point of view and false from another is a valuable realization. Working with texts from different viewpoints is one way of starting to develop this critical reading skill.

One worker filled out an accident report form when a box of shoes fell off a shelf and hit her on the head at work. The final question on the form asked "What will you do in the future to prevent this accident from happening again?" Almost any given response would seem to point to employee responsibility for the accident. Understanding the greater implications of the forms we fill out, and how they will impact our future is valuable.

Another interesting exercise is looking at euphemisms and the ways that words are used at work. What implications do workers see for using the term "bus boys" referring to men, "temporaries" referring to long-term workers who do not get benefits, "Chinese" referring to all people of Southeast Asian descent, or "headcount reduction" referring to firings? What other euphemisms are used in their workplace? What is their purpose? Workers may come up with their own alternative words which reflect the truth more accurately.

Rewriting Company Documents in Clear English

The fact that bureaucratized, indecipherable texts are the sort most commonly encountered in the workplace gives further reason why reading is a skill deemed unimportant by workers (Joliffe, 1997). The exclusionary language style that keeps workers from obtaining information essential to their health and safety is problematic. It is necessary that the communicative practices of the workplace including signage, documentation, oral communication, and other language uses become adapted to the needs and practices of new language learners. One of the prime examples of bad writing is incomprehensible corporatese. For example, I taught in one manufacturing plant where about 80% of its workforce was low-level non-native speakers of English and native speakers with less than a high school education. The company management regularly wrote policies for this intended audience which appear intentionally incomprehensible, for example, "Effective immediately, in accordance with the Illinois Clean Air Act, the utilization of tobacco products on these premises is strictly prohibited." The class discussion of this policy allowed new English learners to inquire why management did not simply write "No Smoking."

At another company, a poster explaining what to do if someone is choking is displayed in the lunchroom where we hold reading classes. It reads: "Apply subdiaphragmatic abdominal thrusts (the Heimlich maneuver) until the foreign body is expelled." One hopes that those helping the choking victim have a good dictionary handy. An excellent way to avoid these confusing messages is to encourage employees to have a voice in the way materials are written. Worker involvement in rewriting company documents is not only an empowering literacy activity

(Rhoder & French, 1994) but also a demonstration of common sense to those who would choose to confuse rather than enlighten their readers. Rewriting documents in plain English is a reasonable accommodation toward communication and involving learners with rewriting company documents and changing communication practices throughout the workplace can be a valuable means of including all workers in the organizational culture. Workers become empowered as they begin to view themselves as both consumers and creators of text (Rosow, 1995).

WORKPLACE IMPROVEMENT PROJECTS

Becoming active participants in workplace change is a big step for workers who may have long felt that only their bodies were required at their jobs, not their minds. This is often a learning process for all sides as employers realize that workers offering ideas may not fit within their preconceived notions of propriety and all parties learn to listen, dialogue, and negotiate. Improvement projects provide immediate transfer of learning from the classroom to the job. There are a number of activities in which learners may engage to use their new communication skills in making workplace improvements. These activities may begin in the class as speaking or writing exercises, but can be brought out into the workplace as they begin to feel more comfortable. Encourage students to exchange the roles of supervisor and coworker and to give and receive feedback on how to use vocabulary, body language, and tone in different situations. They may also practice the complexities of stating, explaining, supporting, and justifying their position in the face of opposition. There is an art to phrasing suggestions, explanations, and requests in ways that are more likely to achieve our goals, which must be practiced. Workers conditioned to accept given orders, explanations, and instructions unquestioningly may need to learn new critical-thinking skills to participate successfully in a changing workplace where input is valued more than blind obedience. They also need to consider the consequences of questioning authority in situations where input is less welcomed.

Examples of Communicative Practices
for Role Plays and Writing Exercises

- Apologies
- Descriptions
- Disputes
- Explanations
- Inquiries
- Instructions
- Reprimands
- Requests
- Warnings

In class, try to use the style of language that workers are likely to hear at work. Insisting on hypercorrect textbook English usage such as "May I?" instead of "Can I?" or "To whom shall I give this?" rather than "Who gets this?" seldom helps learners' daily communication needs. However it is important to explain that register, such as degree of politeness, formality, or use of slang can change according to the context. The casual banter between coworkers may be very different from the language expected when dealing with executives or school officials. Give learners the opportunity to try different language styles by offering a variety of authentic writing exercises.

Examples of Writing Exercises

- Write an article for the company newsletter about a class achievement.
- Write a memo inviting people to join the soccer team or other social group.
- Thank coworkers in a memo or note for their efforts in speaking more slowly.
- Create a brochure to tell coworkers about the literacy classes.
- Write a letter to the local newspaper about a current issue.

Assignments in which learners can go out and about, asking questions and researching problems to gather information are an excellent way to begin using their skills. A valuable exercise is to have them conduct a little research to find out information about their own organization (Auerbach & Wallerstein, 1987).

Examples of Research Assignments

- Generate questions about a current work problem and survey coworkers.
- Interview someone about his or her job.
- Find out who has worked here the longest, and ask how things have changed.
- Find out how many customers we serve each day or how many parts we produce.
- Find out how many accidents we had last year and their causes.
- Find out job titles and responsibilities to create an organizational chart.

By honing their skills both in and outside of the class, workers can begin to participate more fully in understanding and changing their organization.

Offering Suggestions and Making Improvements

Many organizations encourage employee input in suggesting ways to improve profitability, performance and safety. Some even have suggestion boxes or programs where employees are rewarded for submitting ideas for improvements. One way to begin to elicit suggestions as a writing exercise can be a simple sentence completion worksheet with sentence starters.

Examples of Making Improvements, Sentence Starters

- If I were the president of this organization I would change __ _____
- The best part of my job is _____
- The worst thing about my job is _____
- My job would be safer if _____

- My job would be better if _____
- The thing I worry about most at work is _____
- If I could have any job here, I would be a _____ because _____
- We could improve communication here by _____ _____

   In some organizations we first brainstorm about ways we could increase production, reduce scrap, and improve safety and then practice writing these in the format required on the suggestion form. We discuss the need to frame our concerns in ways that would benefit the company. When a few of these suggestions were implemented, such as new ventilation fans and lowered machine rates, learners saw the results from filling out the quality and safety improvement forms. At other companies where I have taught, workers are given bonuses if their suggestions are implemented and learners were delighted to find that writing down their ideas in class not only improved their workplaces but was financially rewarding as well. At times, workers may not feel comfortable submitting the letters or memos they have composed in class, and may wish to practice their writing for a while before they create documents that are actually delivered. Respecting their privacy and level of comfort with sharing their writings is essential.

   Workplace improvement projects often spring naturally from class discussions and learners may wish to focus upon improving the conditions for employees. In one company where I taught factory workers, the English classes were held in the office area and the ESL students passed through the office lunchroom before and after class and during breaks. In class they often remarked upon the clean and comfortable amenities available to the office workers including free coffee, a water cooler, and new microwaves. By comparison to the office lunchroom, their own environment in the production area seemed shabby and the appliances were old and in disrepair. They decided to ask for some of the same amenities provided for the office workers in their own work area. The multilevel class began with brainstorming ideas for improvements. Some of the lower level English speakers were able to input just a few words such as "broken" or "dirty" and drew a picture of a rodent to depict the pest, while others explained their concerns in greater detail. As a writing exercise in class, learners came up with numerous suggestions. We used dictionaries to look up unfamiliar words and check spelling. They asked for my assistance with some grammar and punctuation issues and then we wrote up their suggestions in the form of a memo and presented them to the plant manager.

ESL Class Suggestions for Improvements Memo

We need paper towels in the lunchroom because if you spill something you can't clean it. Sometimes people spill the food on the table and that is why the tables are dirty.

We need a new microwave or two in the lunchroom. One microwave is not working.

The door does not work. When you close it, the door does not open again.

We need cold water to drink in the lunchroom.

We need cold water to drink in Compression.

Some of the refrigerators do not work well. They are not very cold.

Some people leave spoiled food in the refrigerators. They need to be cleaned, they are too dirty.

We need more towels and soap in the bathrooms.

Some people have seen a rat in front of the bathroom.

The bathrooms are dirty. We need someone to clean the bathrooms every day.

There are not enough bathrooms for everybody.

Smoking should be in a different area, not by the lockers. It makes our clothes smell bad.

The plant manager wrote back to us with a comment after each suggestion explaining how it was being addressed, and we read these in class together. The company had quickly addressed the majority of the class's concerns. Towel dispensers were installed in the bathrooms and lunch area, a new microwave was purchased, pest control was called in, refrigerators were cleaned, and the bathrooms were painted, washed, and waxed. Students were enthusiastic and expressed feeling empowered by the changes implemented. Composing a thank you note to show appreciation for such changes is another writing experience that learners can practice.

While many of workers' environmental concerns at this company were addressed by management, others, such as vending machine problems ("They are sometimes robbers, they take the money but they don't give a drink"), lack of drinking water, parking concerns, and burns from hot machinery were discussed in class where workers came up with alternative solutions that they shared with one another. Parking far away from the dust receptacles minimized dirt on cars, and moving cars during break after 5:00 p.m. to the office lot were suggestions created to avoid vandalism and grime. Writing notes to the vending machine attendant about refunds and bringing one's own soda or coffee to work were suggestions for dealing with other irritations. One learner suggested cutting the feet off socks and pulling them over their forearms to protect their skin from burns. At other companies workers developed techniques such as heating their lunches on work machinery to compensate for insufficient microwaves. These varied and creative responses to problems are the result of an urgent and real need to use language to communicate.

Health and Safety

Discussions of health and safety often occur informally in class as people discuss their own injuries or health problems. Once in class I happened to glance at a learner who was holding his left hand oddly cradled in his right. There were four or five ugly, deep cuts across the back of his swollen hand which looked infected with yellow pus. "Geraldo," I exclaimed, "What happened to your hand?" He shrugged. "Did that happen here at work?" He nodded. "Did the machine close on your hand?" Another nod. "Did you go to the doctor?" He shook his head. The wounds looked as if they needed stitches. "When did this happen?" "*Miércoles,*" he replied softly. Five days ago. The other Spanish-speaking students began to question him. "Why didn't you go to the clinic? Do you have insurance? Then you should get a tetanus shot. You should go to the doctor." Geraldo shrugged and hid his hand under the table, looking down.

I was told later by another student that Geraldo was afraid to report the accident because he had deliberately rigged his machine to override the safety guard in order to work faster. This was not an unusual behavior, though technically forbidden. Many illegal and unsafe practices were tacitly approved by supervisors who looked the other way when workers cheated by overriding safety devices, taking off personal protective equipment, ignoring safety procedures, or working without documentation. These activities were all common practices and advantageous to management. Yet workers were also well aware that they alone would take the full brunt of the punishment should their luck run out. Acknowledging and actually talking about these situations with management instead of playing along with the emperor's new clothes illusion of aboveboard practices can make positive changes possible. People of good will are usually willing to make changes in workplace practices that are unfair or discriminatory, but they may need to be informed or reminded of such practices by those adversely impacted. By bringing issues to their attention in a way that assumes oversight rather than malicious intent, learners are less likely to raise defense mechanisms or anger.

During one brainstorming session workers brought up a number of health and safety issues. Some concerns included irritation and itchiness of their skin and eyes from the plastic material; chemical vapors which caused headaches and coughing; excessive noise from the machines; machines smashing fingers; cuts from knives, sharp pieces of plastic, and sharp metal slivers; and burns from hot machinery. We were able to tie their concerns to readings of the company safety policies as well as reading chemical labels and material safety data sheets to learn more about long-term exposure to products. Discussing employees' responsibilities and the advantages of using safety equipment, speaking up about unsafe situations, and learning about hazardous materials as well as discussing employer responsibilities to provide safety information, eliminate hazards, and supply proper protective equipment are valuable ways to improve workplace safety.

Incorporating Math Skills

Numeracy skills are also valued in the workplace and often taught in conjunction with literacy. There are many exercises that can be used to teach math skills in a meaningful context. Learning how to calculate your pay or count change to make sure you are not being cheated is an important motivation for many learners. Creating charts and graphs of important issues for workers such as employment, immigration, 401K plans, or creating surveys of how many people in class have been injured, laid off, or promoted, or have spoken up at a meeting are exercises that incorporate math in a meaningful way. Using math skills to compare increased errors or accidents that correlate with increased production rates can give workers ammunition in their quest for workplace improvements.

Wages are a common concern discussed in class. A photo-essay written by a learner about one of her long-time "temporary" coworkers who assembles expensive parts by hand, began a discussion about how much money the company made on each part. Workers were often warned by their supervisors and in the company newsletter that the parts they made were very expensive and that worker errors cost the company considerable sums of money. However, there was less emphasis placed on the amount of money the company was earning from workers' labor. As the student showed the class her photo, she pointed to the components: "These parts too expensive, sell for seven dollars each."

"And how many does your friend make every day?" I asked.
"Maybe 2,000, sometimes 3,000," she replied.

As a simple math problem we set up a conservative estimate that the parts she made each day were worth about $14,000. We then calculated her daily wages. The company paid approximately $9 per hour to the labor agency which kept about one third of her wages. As a temporary worker she earned about $6 per hour and worked 8 hours per day. We subtracted taxes and social security to come up with about $40 per day as her average wage. We then discussed how the company spent the remaining $13,928 on expenses such as plastic material, rent, insurance, and office workers' salaries. We also considered the connotations of the word "expensive" used to describe parts. Many workers were apprehensive about working on these jobs because of the pressure of making costly mistakes. We discussed the possibility that when working on expensive pieces, they might proudly view their work as adding value to the parts through their labor instead of just feeling anxious about the amount of money their errors could cost.

Another concern was the change of raises. While one company had previously given a 50-cent per hour raise to all the plant workers each year, under the new policy it had been changed to a 5% raise across the board. Again we performed some basic math calculations in class and found that while the workers who made $7.00 per hour would now only get a 35-cent raise, those making $20.00 per hour would get a full dollar raise. They expressed concern that this was unfair for them as most made less than $9.00 per hour though it was clearly beneficial to the higher paid workers. Calculations such as these, which contribute to tangible understandings of the way money is used, can be very motivational in getting learners interested in improving their math skills.

Hands-on, authentic, and productive action projects in the workplace reinforce literacy skills in reading, writing, and math in a way that simultaneously addresses workers' other needs and promotes organizational change. Providing opportunities for workers to identify problems and work on solutions enhances their confidence and brings awareness of their initiatives throughout the organization. By facilitating the implementation of workplace improvement projects, instructors can foster literacy learning that expands beyond the classroom into concrete improvements in workers' lives.

CHAPTER 5

Exploring Literacy Through Personal Histories and Experiences

Creating an environment in which workers' stories may be shared is the first step in eliciting the personal experiences of learners. It is important to establish an atmosphere of trust in the literacy classroom, to set a tone where it is okay to make mistakes and to speak freely. The instructors act as role models here when they show that they can be fallible and even laugh at their own mistakes. Trying to understand learners' work processes and attempting to learn about students' culture and language (even when occasionally botching the pronunciation) show that the educator is also a learner.

Let the learners know that for the next hour or two this room is our sanctuary—a space apart from the workaday world where we are safe to try out different ideas, to stumble and to help each other back up. Learners aren't afraid to ask for what they need in such a setting. Some classes choose to set ground rules including that the topics discussed in class are confidential and not to be repeated outside. Other classes choose to close the door when controversial topics are brought up so as not to be overheard.

Class traditions such as checking in, sharing food, telling a joke, or reporting a successful literacy experience create a familiar routine. Each class evolves its own personality. While each session is different—there are times when we need to vent our anger and frustration, times when we need to mourn and when we need to celebrate—a comforting pattern of expected and innovative classroom activities helps to break the ice and encourage participation. Offering a quote of the day, a tongue twister, an interesting news story for discussion are some ways of beginning or ending the class session. We often start with an opening check-in to report any important news or personal successes and end with dialogue journal writing, and an informal evaluation of the session with time for questions, complaints, and validations.

The key to learner-centeredness is acknowledging, welcoming, and building on learners' concerns rather than dismissing them as interruption of the class. A good rule for workplace basic skills programs is if it's not interesting and enjoyable you're not doing it right. Not that there aren't disappointing days and dry spells or occasional bouts of frustration and drudgery, but most of the time it is great fun. If the teacher feels bored or irritated during the class there is a good chance that the learners do as well.

MOTIVATIONS FOR LEARNERS

Workers may be motivated to participate in literacy programs for a variety of reasons. Besides the opportunity to advance or improve their current work situation, many people want to improve their literacy skills for survival needs outside of work, in order to help their children or as a means of sharing their own stories and culture with others. By understanding and incorporating these motivations within the program, learner retention and achievement is enhanced.

Addressing Literacy Needs Outside of Work

While on-the-job reading skills are important to many workers, their responsibilities outside of work as parents, consumers, and citizens may have even more demanding literacy requirements. Dealing with bureaucracies, managing finances, and being involved with their children's schooling are just a few of the situations in which we need strong literacy skills to participate adequately. Healthcare is a common concern in this country and workers often discuss the policies of their insurance plans and their quests to find doctors that speak their language. A common problem mentioned in class is when learners (or an interpreter) call their physician's office they are often told they can not have an appointment to see the doctor for several weeks or more. To address this, we practice mock telephone calls, stating phrases that emphasize the seriousness of their illnesses: "No that's no good. I am very sick, I need to see a doctor right away." Many learners do not realize that it is acceptable and often necessary to be assertive in dealing with healthcare providers in this country. Sharing stories about their health experiences produces knowledge about the practices of the U.S. healthcare system as well as alternative remedies from their home cultures available for the minor injuries and headaches that many suffer at work.

Encourage learners to bring in authentic materials from home such as fliers, forms, magazines, coupons, newspaper articles, report cards, recipes, letters, tax forms, prescription labels, maps, and instructions. I bring in my own credit card notices, election fliers, and junk mail. Discussions of these real materials can include what they are used for, and why they are or are not important. Ask: "Who reads these materials"? "Who seeks the help of family and friends to read them"? The U.S. values of independence and being able to read materials by oneself may not be as highly valued in cultures which stress interdependence and cultural cohesion. They may prefer to have a relative translate in exchange for cooking food or babysitting; these types of exchanges reinforce community and family ties. In the workplace as well, seeking the help of others in writing and reading can build relationships. Finding out what learners would like to be able to do by themselves is better than assuming that they have an interest in being able to perform specific tasks alone, such as filling out census forms.

For ESL students, dealing with the Immigration and Naturalization Service (INS) can be confusing and problematic and is often an important focus for their reading, writing, and speaking skills. Once when we were discussing fire safety, a student remarked, "We never had a fire drill, but one time when immigration came, everybody evacuated the building!" This led to

discussions of immigration policies, the long wait and high fees
to become a citizen, the difficulty of the test, and the labyrinth
of forms, applications, and procedures needed to complete the
process. One student brought in a letter stating the reasons that
his application for citizenship had been denied, and we struggled
together to translate the legalese of the rejection form letter. We
discussed the issues of documented versus undocumented workers, who benefits from undocumented labor, and how. Students
took out their green cards, remarking on the irony, "They're
not green," and passed them around the classroom while they
shared information about their immigration status and regulations. Though they worked hard and paid taxes, many seemed
unable to navigate the barriers surrounding the benefits of full
citizenship. Offering citizenship classes at work can be one way
of meeting learners' needs in this area.

Workers may be wary of revealing their undocumented
status until they know the instructor and their classmates very
well. Students often joke, "You're not going to turn this in to
the INS are you?" when I ask them to relate stories of how they
came to this country. When I assured one long-time class that I
wouldn't use their real names in writing about them, they
laughed, "These aren't our real names anyway!" One group of
workers related that a coworker had been badly injured while
lifting heavy boxes on the job and was now unable to work.

"But doesn't he collect workers' comp?" I asked naively.

They shook their heads, "No, he gets nothing."

"But there are laws!" I protested.

"Yes *maestra*, there are laws that say we should not work
in this country."

These common interchanges shed light on the difficulties
faced by immigrant laborers who arrive in this country without
documentation. The use of the term "illegal alien" suggests not
only that immigrants are somehow less than human; but that
their quest to come to the United States and work hard in much
needed labor is somehow morally reprehensible as well. These
immigrant workers face discrimination, fear, and shame because they are denied the right to work here legally.

Another practical issue many second-language learners report is that telephone conversations, because they lack the visual cues and feedback of face-to-face communication, are particularly difficult and nerve-wracking for them. Practicing telephone calls can be a valuable way to overcome these fears. Students often ask me to call the pharmacy or school for them, and rehearsing likely scripts and making real calls in a supportive environment can be helpful. When no one wanted to call for the pizza the last day of class, we practiced the phrase "I would like a large pepperoni with cheese," giving the address and asking how much it would cost. However during the actual call when the clerk unexpectedly asked, "Would you like garlic bread with that?" the student panicked and thrust the phone at me.

Crime is another serious issue that can be a very real fear for low-wage workers who often live in dangerous neighborhoods. Students have related in class their experiences of having their homes robbed, being held up at gunpoint, having tires slashed and being afraid of the gang members in their neighborhoods. This fear is often compounded by a mistrust of police, stemming from experiences with corrupt law enforcement officials in their own countries or negative experiences that they have had in this country. Using a lesson such as "What to do if you are stopped by the police" (English Literacy and Civics Education Project, 2001) can open discussions about differing cultural perceptions of the police, appropriate responses, and learners' experiences with the law.

Low-literate adults may be limited in the geographic areas they dare to venture into, preferring the familiarity of their own neighborhood. A group field trip can give them the experience of venturing into new areas in a non-threatening way. Visiting a library, courthouse, community college lecture, city hall meeting, or PTA meeting can be very educational and help learners to feel more comfortable in visiting these places on their own. Even fun trips like baseball games, museum, or zoo visits offer excellent opportunities for reading signs, maps, and even keeping score cards.

One day in class, a worker requested that we practice spelling the names of numbers so that she could write out checks. Many of the learners had never written checks before, relying instead on family members or using high-fee currency exchanges for their financial transactions. Literacy students may live in neighborhoods with few banks. A man who did not have a checking account wrote in his dialogue journal about being tired from walking long distances to pay his bills in cash. Some women reported that their husbands wrote all the checks for their families. Another learner brought in a letter for me to help her read about a water deposit required for her village, and she showed me the check she had written which had several errors painted over with correction fluid. I told her she could not "white out" mistakes on a check and would need to write a new one. She was surprised and thought this seemed wasteful. One woman laughed as she related that when she got her first paycheck she did not know what it was. "Where is money?" she had asked. We practiced writing mock checks for about an hour and several people commented that this lesson had been particularly valuable. Other consumer education about buying a house, credit reports, and interest rates may be helpful. Visiting a bank or having a representative come to speak can be another good way to learn more about finances.

Studying religious texts can be a further motivation for learning English (Purcell-Gates & Waterman, 2000). One student told me she wanted to learn English so that when she was dying, she would be able to understand an English-speaking priest giving the last rites if necessary. Another man related that his Bible study group met at a different house each week and required the host to read a verse out loud. He always asked his wife to read but he wanted to practice reading for this purpose and always volunteered to read aloud in front of the class. Providing opportunities for learners to achieve such goals enhances their literacy practice.

Children

The primary purpose for many adults to start and stay in literacy programs is to help the children in their lives (Yaffe & Williams, 1998). Improving their literacies is seen as a key to opening educational doors for their kids. They want to be able to participate fully in parent-teacher conferences, helping with homework, reading stories together, going to the library, and using computers. They often mention their concerns of keeping up with their children's learning. Adults who improve their own literacy also have a positive impact on the education of the children in their lives (Paratore, 2001). By learning more, they are better prepared to assist with their children's educational needs and they serve as role models who use text confidently and are lifelong learners.

While most family literacy programs help parents to assist their children's literacy, for adult ESL learners their children's literacy quickly surpasses their own and the roles are very different, if not reversed. One Albanian student invited her 15-year-old son to come to class to help her. Sporting baggy jeans and a peach fuzz moustache, he looked and acted like a typical American teenager with only a hint of an accent to give him away. He seemed awkward yet cocky about being the English liaison for his mother and came to our class to help on days when he was not working after school at a drug store. He often volunteered to read aloud in class and helped the other students with their writing and seemed more patient with the other students than with his mother. If scheduling makes it feasible, including workers' children or spouses in the literacy program can be an added incentive to participate. Using homework assignments or a class web page that workers can share with their children or grandchildren are great ways of fostering intergenerational learning. Talking about how U.S. school systems work and what schools expect of parents as well as bringing in report cards or role playing parent-teacher conferences are also valuable lessons requested by adults with school-age children.

Balancing the fears of losing their ethnic identities through assimilation versus being excluded from the opportunities of mainstream American culture leads some immigrants to inconsistent attitudes toward native language usage by their children. Though they generally agree that it is important for their children to learn English, there are differences of opinion about when, where, and how this should come about. One learner forbade her older children to speak English to the baby because he might get confused. Some argue adamantly that they want their children in mainstream English classes, not bilingual programs, while others feel that their kids will be at a disadvantage if not allowed to speak their native languages in school. Many immigrants express dismay that their children can no longer speak their first languages properly and have become too reliant on English. It is harder for these adults to adjust to the new language and culture than it is for their children, who readily embrace American fashions, music, and slang.

Learners also report that their children's support of their parents' language learning was sometimes ambivalent. Children often express a desire to have their parents speak English. One woman showed me a list of 10 words her daughter had dictated for writing practice with the orders: "Listen" and "Study for test Mom!" While children help their parents with their homework, even coming with them to class, they are often impatient with their slow progress, expressing frustration and amusement at their errors. They even at times seemed reluctant to relinquish the power of the sole transmitter of information from the Anglo world. The power of being the only one in the family who can understand report cards, field English telephone calls, and use the computer gives these youngsters an elevated status which might be minimized by parental language acquisition. However, children also feel the extra burden of having to be available to translate for their parents and take on extra responsibilities. Some workers bring their kids along to the office to help interpret benefits programs and insurance options, and though young children might be fluently bilingual, it is difficult for them to grasp the complexities of copayments, 401K plans, and W-2 forms during these meetings.

Sharing Cultural and Ethnic History

In many classes, discussion and writings about cultural differences and journeys are frequent topics and a focus for literacy activities. Many times learners don't want to focus on filling out

forms, instead they wish to improve their language skills in order to tell their grandchildren about their family history and
escape from the homeland as well as sharing their cultural pride
and beliefs with coworkers.

To begin such discussions I sometimes pass around photo
books about learners' neighborhoods and their home countries.
A woman with limited English skills excitedly pointed to a picture of people harvesting rice in Vietnam: "*I* worked in the rice
fields." Learners are often very interested in looking at the pictures of familiar scenes from their home countries and new
neighborhoods and to share and point out their area of origin
on maps. Using a time line to write the years of major life events
is also a simple tool for helping learners' to relate their life histories and cultural experiences.

Fleeing war and poverty while leaving their families and
homelands behind are frequent topics for immigrants in class.
Many cite the reason that they came to the United States was to
find a better life for their children. Opportunities for education
are valued and mentioned often. Some of the stories shared were
funny or touching, but many were sad. One man shared the
story of his escape from Vietnam and how 30 people died during
the boat ride to the Philippines without food or water. Another
related the humiliation she felt after she escaped Vietnam and
arrived in Hong Kong where they shaved her head and put her
in a refugee camp. There were sometimes tears and silence as
these difficult stories were told. New language learners are often
disarmingly honest as they relate their experiences. They still
lack the "weasel words" that allow us to circumlocute and
euphemize in our first languages.

Most immigrants agree that they are happy to find work
in the United States, but there are many tradeoffs to leaving their
homelands. One woman said, "When I arrived here, I feel sad.
I cry. I miss my mother. I don't know language. I stay home, no
job, no money. Now, I happy when I working." Another remarked that she liked the communication in the United States
because everyone has telephones, but she did not like the snow
and the gangs. She missed her family and friends, fresh food,
and having parties outside without police interference, but she

did not miss the politics, insecurity, and unclean hospitals that she left behind in Mexico.

A recurring topic which emerges from conversations and writings about photographs is cultural comparisons of their native countries with the United States. One woman wrote that in Vietnam "the neighborhood helps with baby, have long vacation New Year, but I don't have freedom, I don't like no jobs, government don't help people handicapped, no washrooms." Another commented that in Vietnam it is friendly because you know everyone in your neighborhood but in the United States people feel afraid because they don't know their neighbors. One student brought in some Vietnamese money and we discussed the difference in wages between the United States and other countries. She reported that most people she knows in Vietnam earn about $1.50 per day. Supporting overseas relatives financially is a big concern shared by many immigrants. Trying to make ends meet here while sending enough money to help their families abroad was a large responsibility, but most indicate that they feel proud that they are able to help their families financially.

STRATEGIES FOR LEARNING

There are several learning strategies which can be incorporated into learner-centered programs is order to engage workers in meaningful literacy activities. These include encouraging discussions, encoding themes, writing stories, reading a variety of materials, corresponding in dialogue journals, playfully learning through games and jokes, and publishing learners' stories.

Discussions

Discussions are both the precursors and constant companions of text-based literacy activities. Talking in class about issues of importance sets the stage for reading and writing activities. Experiencing the connection between oral and written stories helps workers to view texts as living and creative acts rather than faultless tomes handed down from authorities above. Providing time for discussion also encourages learners to debate issues, to persuade, and even be persuaded as they deal with differences of opinion in constructive ways.

Invite guest speakers from within the company to talk to the class in order to provide a less stressful arena for asking in-depth questions than is possible at most official meetings. In one company we invited the quality manager to make a presentation to our class to explain component blueprints, schematic drawings consisting primarily of symbols and numbers which were not well understood by workers. This gave them the opportunity to ask questions about the documents and talk about related work processes in a more relaxed environment than the busy factory floor. Additionally, inviting guest speakers from the community including schools, police departments, voter registration programs, domestic violence shelters, or other areas which workers deem important adds to the class dialogues.

ESL classroom conversations may slip easily back and forth from English to first languages. Sometimes a topic will begin in English but as excitement mounts, it quickly switches to first-language arguments until protests from the other students of "English, English!" pull it back to a common language. Though the discussions often become heated, the interest generated by controversial themes creates contagious communication in which lower-level students can literally "borrow a phrase" heard from one of their peers and capture it (if only in short-term memory) in order to make their own opinions known. However, there are sometimes difficulties balancing respect for students' first languages with the need to communicate as a group. Classes may elect to set their own rules for language use. Some choose to have penalties for speaking first languages in the classroom while others encourage bilingualism.

Although our classes may be titled "English as a Second Language," many students already speak more than two languages fluently. Reinforcing the value of their multilingualism and multiculturalism rather than focusing only upon their imperfect grasp of English is important. A Vietnamese woman wrote a photo-essay about one of her Mexican coworkers who taught her Spanish: "She is a good friend. Sometimes she talks in her language. She teaches, I learn Spanish. I am very happy because I speak her language at work." During a lesson on ordinal numbers she proudly said, "My first language is Vietnamese, my second language is Chinese, my third language is English and my fourth language is Spanish!" The predominant language of the workplace may not be English and workers of all nationalities pick up the most frequently used phrases, often entering the classroom with the Spanish greeting, "*Buenos dias. Cómo está?*" And regardless of linguistic background everyone seems to know the familiar workers' lament, "*Mucho trabajo, poco dinero*" (Much work, little money).

As they tell their stories and offer insights, it is fascinating to watch the social interactions and personal relationships developing in class. Conversations somehow cross lines of culture and illuminate the working friendships which form in spite of language differences through the shared companionship and struggles of working immigrants. This builds a sense of community for workers from different departments and language groups. Though there are frequently miscommunications and differences, we try to transcend them with humor and patience.

In a major cultural faux pas, I once touched the head of a Vietnamese student when commenting on how much I liked his new haircut. Although I knew that it was very disrespectful in his culture to touch the top of someone's head, I was not thinking about it until he flinched and pulled away, giving me a disgusted look. I immediately realized what I had done and apologized profusely. Then, recognizing this as a teachable moment, I began asking about what gestures and body language were acceptable and unacceptable in their different cultures. This led to an interesting discussion about who and where it was permissible to touch and what different gestures signify. Unfortunately, a few of the students learned from this lesson that a really good way to irritate the Vietnamese was to touch the tops of their heads and then run away laughing.

Drawing out learners and gaining their involvement in discussions can be facilitated by asking questions designed to engage them: "How do you feel about this?" and "What is your opinion?" can be used to engage non-participative members and "That's interesting, tell us more about it," encourages expansion of ideas. The educator can also help in discussions by leading learners to consider other facets of an issue: "That's one way of looking at it, but what would happen if . . . ?"

Encoding Learners' Themes

Taking the themes that learners have discussed and transforming the problems posed during discussions is an important step in developing a critical perspective on learner-centered activities. By transforming the topics from a conversation into a different form such as a picture, song, story, or written script, the instructor may both expand and reconfigure the issues in order to engage learners from a different angle. The instructor may write short dialogues, which Auerbach and Wallerstein (1987) refer to as "codes," in order to expand some of the discussion topics initiated by the class. By working with their ideas and themes, the educator is able to add new vocabulary words and grammatical structures as well as open the topics to further discussion. These written dialogues which expand some of the themes generated by the class are echoes of the learners' own conversations used to generate further discussion on controversial topics. A few details are usually changed to remove the situations from their specific context, but students recognize the gist of the experiences related in the codifications. "Is same for me!" a student exclaimed after we read a code about the difficulties of spouses working different shifts. Others made similar comments as we read codes about children helping with translation, learning about computers, receiving demerit points, and supervisors' impatience with attempts to speak English. Some of the topics generated included working two jobs, coping with the heat in the plant, balancing overtime and family time, and finding opportunities to practice English. Here are two examples.

Talking at Work

Thao and Juan are talking at work.

Thao: What was your first job, Juan?

Juan: My first job was on a farm in my country before I came to the United States. It was my father's farm and my brothers and sisters and I all worked on the farm to help him. I was in school for only three years because I was working when I was young.

Thao: My first job was on a farm too, in Vietnam. I liked the work because it was outside. When I came to this country, it was hard to get used to working in a factory. Now I want to go to school to learn more English but I have to work too many hours. Do you take English classes?

Juan: Yes. I have English classes at work. I learn a little bit, but it is difficult. I need to practice talking, but my friends and family all speak Spanish.

Thao: All my friends and family speak Vietnamese.

1. What do you think Juan and Thao can do to help each other learn English?

2. Why can it be difficult to learn English?

3. What are some things you do to practice your English?

4. Who are some people at work and in your neighborhood that you can practice with?

Computers

Tom: I just bought a new computer for my son. He can use it to do his homework for school. But I don't know how to use it. Do you use a computer, Ann?

Ann: Sometimes I use the computer at the library. I can get the news from my country in my language. I can send e-mail to my sister in Texas, too. It is interesting. I like it. My children use the computers at school to play games and study.

Tom: My supervisor uses a computer at work. He says it is easy, but I wonder if I am too old to learn all of that. Maybe my son can show me how to use the computer.

1. How do you feel about learning to use a computer?

2. Do you have a computer at home?

3. Do you use a computer at work?

4. Does your family use a computer?

5. What can your family and friends do with a computer?

Wallerstein (1983) recommends having more advanced students act out the role-plays to help the beginners understand. She also suggests the following questions to generate dialogue about codes:

1. What do you see? (To identify basic vocabulary)

2. What is the problem here? (To find the conflict)

3. Do you also experience this? How do you feel about it? (To personalize the topic)

4. Why is there a problem? (To look at the larger cultural or historical perspective)

5. What can we do? (To generate alternatives and solutions)

Writing Our Stories

For beginning writers the task of constructing an entire story from scratch may feel overwhelming. Providing them with samples in which they may copy some of the structures or outlines can help to ease them into more independent writing. A structure such as the one below can be used to help learners relate their personal experiences with overcoming obstacles:

I wanted	because	but	so I

Other story starters can be used to begin class discussions and develop them into written stories that are shared with the class.

Story Starters

1. My first job was_____

2. I am happiest when I_____

3. I feel proud when I_____

4. I am really good at_____

5. I'll never forget when_____

6. When I started this job_____but now_____

7. I used to believe_____but now I feel_____

8. I love_____ because_____

9. The best part of my job is_____

10. I get angry when_____

Even short quotations can be a great source for provoking learners' thoughts. Beginning class with a quote on the board can start conversations about the vocabulary and deeper meanings of the quotations. An Internet search of "labor quotations" or "work quotations" can provide many online reference sources. Quotes such as, "When a man tells you that he got rich through hard work, ask him: 'Whose?'" (Don Marquis from www.quotationspage.com), or "Society cares for the individual only so far as he is profitable." (Simone De Beavoir from www.absolutefacts.com) may elicit strong responses. Asking learners if they agree or disagree with the author's sentiment and how their personal experiences have impacted their beliefs can be the start for interesting discussions, stories, and writing exercises.

Priming the Writing Process with Example Stories

Having learners create and read their own texts is an excellent starting point for beginning readers. Moving into reading the words of others affords opportunities for inspiration, critical discussions, and experiencing the pleasure of reading. I have found that using texts which are transcriptions of spoken language such as *Gig: Americans Talk about Their Jobs* (Bowe, Bowe, & Streeter, 2000) or the classic *Working* by Studs Terkel (1997) are good starting points for new readers. They are easier to read because rhythms and vocabulary are truer to the language that we speak and hear daily than the literary conventions of written language which are further from our lived experiences (Purcell-Gates, 1995).

Offering an overview of high interest popular literature is a way of engaging learners and helping them to find genres that they can read for pleasure. Introducing an excerpt of a different style each week and providing a variety of books to borrow can expand learner's horizons. Exposure to various genres of literature including sci-fi, mystery, romance, children's literature, and comic books may be used to explore cultural themes and discover learners' own literary preferences (Krashen, 2001). Additionally, exposure to nonfiction genres including self-help, biography, tabloids, special interest magazines, newspapers, and history give a glimpse of the wide array of available reading material and writing styles.

Using a commercially produced workbook as a supplement is a common option in workplace literacy programs. It is sometimes difficult for instructors and learners to create a curriculum based entirely on learners' own materials if they haven't done it before. A standard textbook can offer supplemental reading and grammar material and a little break from addressing the unrelenting barrage of real world concerns. There are high interest collections of true stories, poems, and fiction available as well as grammar-based texts available. Some learners love to practice penmanship and spelling and I usually give them extra handouts to practice these at home. Other classes like to read poems, magazines about their industry, or the local paper.

Writing in response to a story that they have read is one way of seeding learners' stories when they believe that they have nothing to write about. I also find it important to write while my students are writing and to share my own life stories as I ask them to relate theirs. One class insisted that I write my essay in Spanish to be at an equal disadvantage and gleefully marked all of my errors. I also share the stories of other learners with their permission.

Writing about overcoming obstacles infuses pride and recognition in one's own strength and resources. Learners have shared their experiences in standing up to a bully at work, immigrating to a new country, marrying a spouse of a different ethnicity, and asking for a raise as compelling stories about their own experiences with surmounting barriers. Because we seldom see the writings of others in an unfinished state, it is difficult to envision the reworkings and revisions that must be completed before a work comes to light.

The link of the literacy task to a topic that is important to the learner is of utmost importance to their ability to succeed. In one class I hesitated asking learners to write a personal narrative because they seemed to be struggling so much with the required exercise of correctly spelling the days of the weeks and months. However their skill levels jumped dramatically when we began the high interest activity of sharing their immigration experiences. Using the Language Experience Approach in which the instructor writes down learners' dictated stories about important events provides an opportunity for beginning level readers and writers to gain confidence as they read their own words in print.

Instructors must resist the urge to make red marks all over

learners' papers and to circle every error that they make. It is very disheartening to see the outpourings of one's soul reduced to an enumeration of errors. This seemingly insensitive response to sincere communication makes learners self-conscious and unwilling to share. Discuss the content of their writings first focusing on what they are trying to communicate, then you may choose one or two points such as punctuation, grammar, or spelling to focus upon as part of a lesson. Having the learners read their stories aloud while the instructor transcribes them on the board is another way to make corrections unobtrusively.

Dialogue Journals

Dialogue journals are an ongoing written conversation between the learner and the instructor. During each class the student writes a short personal reflection and the instructor responds in writing. Small notebooks which are passed back and forth serve this purpose well. This is a wonderful way to start or end the class session so that students can privately correspond with the instructor about their experiences. In addition to providing practice for writing skills, the journals give voice to some of the quieter students who are less vocal in class (Haas, Smoke, & Hernandez, 1991) and allow teachers to see events from the learners' points of view (Linder & Elish-Piper, 1995). By mirroring and unobtrusively making corrections in their responses, the instructor begins to communicate with learners on a new level. Remember that the primary purpose of dialogue journaling is communication, not correction.

In one class a Latino worker initially resisted writing in his dialogue journal. After a couple of days with no writing in his journal, I told him to go ahead and write in Spanish. He eloquently filled a whole page explaining that he did not understand very much in class. He explained in Spanish that he had never attended English classes and did not know the letters in English. He seemed to be under the mistaken impression that the other students did understand everything. I wrote back to him in English with Spanish translations after each line and he replied in Spanish. The breakthrough came more than halfway through the program when he responded to my inquiry of what he had done over the weekend: *"Durante el fin de semana yo hablé por* <u>telephone</u> *con* <u>my family</u> *y también fue a cenar y* <u>look</u> <u>TV</u> *y estudie un poco."* He continued to write primarily in Spanish but inserted a few English words that he had learned. After a few more weeks, he was writing short phrases in English. Other learners use their journals as a safe venue for describing their feelings about learning, problems at work, and suggestions for improving the class.

Other Fun Activities

Beyond writings and discussions about the often weighty issues of learners' lives are the more playful activities of riddles, jokes, games, and puzzles. These forms of entertainment can be fun ways to practice and help learners to develop the confidence to use their language through nonthreatening activities. Games based on vocabulary and grammar reviews such as bingo, charades, and board games are pleasant ways of reinforcing some of the necessary foundations of literacy.

One of my classes regularly performed magic tricks and took turns telling jokes in English. Introducing simple jokes such as "What has four wheels and flies? A garbage truck" can be used to introduce homophones, synonyms, and humorous conventions as well as opening the doors to having learners try to translate jokes from their own countries. This can be an interesting and difficult task when puns and cultural constructs are often the basis for humor and do not translate well. Also, students may relate their own off-color jokes and this offers the opportunity (to the extent which the class feels comfortable), to discuss often taboo, but important topics. We have spent time laughing, practicing, and being embarrassed over the phonetic differences between "beach" and "bitch," "sheet," and "shit" which are very difficult distinctions for some non-English speakers to discern and pronounce. Although many educators may feel more comfortable avoiding potentially offensive language, it can be a valuable lesson to teach the propriety of using such language and being able to understand it when it is used against them. Specialized texts such as *Dangerous English* (Claire, 1998) are a good reference source for such phrases. In one class a shy young Mexican woman kept asking me the meanings for very explicit sexual terms. I asked her where she was hearing these and she confided that her supervisor said these things to her. Be aware that profane language can be used as sexual and racial harassment in the workplace. However, it is also important to realize that the polite and sanitary language of the office is much different from the linguistic conventions of the shop floor where profanity can be a socially accepted form of communication.

Publishing and Sharing Workers' Stories

Getting workers' writings out of the classroom and into the hands of a larger audience can be a great activity for validating learning and experiences as well as promoting the workplace literacy program within the organization and community. Public readings of workers' stories, dramatic skits, or plays performed in the workplace, publishing booklets of stories, putting them on the world wide web, or producing a CD of workers reading their stories aloud are inexpensive and effective ways of reaching outside audiences. Developing their family histories, creating family trees, or writing autobiographical narratives are means of communicating their stories intergenerationally. Producing newsletters, creating resource guides to services in the community, printing up posters of learners' poems, or performing songs that they have written are additional ways of reaching out to the greater community.

By providing workers with the opportunity to meet their current literacy needs, share their experiences, reinforce their learning through games, find inspiration in the writings of others, and share their newfound literacy talents to audiences outside of the workplace classroom, basic skills programs may go beyond teaching workers, to aiding them in empowering themselves.

CHAPTER 6

Enhancing Literacy with Visual Imagery

Visual imagery, including photography, video, drawing, and other multi-media expressions, are valuable tools for creating a learner-centered curriculum. By integrating a wide variety of learning activities involving visual, auditory, tactile-kinesthetic, affective, and social abilities, literacy classes can most effectively draw on the multiple learning styles and interests of workers. Especially for learners who have rejected (or been rejected by) traditional schooling, accessing literacy through a visual door can be a surprising and successful approach.

Photography is an exciting means of gathering relevant visual images to use in class discussions and writings. It allows workers to document their lives, provides a concrete basis for communicating, and validates the experiences and culture of learners by making them visible. Because low-income workers seldom see themselves portrayed in mainstream media at all, let alone in a positive or realistic manner, they may feel a great need to create their own images. By encouraging learners to represent themselves with their own words and images instead of accepting the representations created by the dominant culture, educators can provide opportunities for better understanding and transformative changes in and outside of the workplace.

Using photographs can also improve the rapport-building process as instructors and learners get to know one another and it involves workers critically in the learning process. Additionally, the use of photos encourages more detailed and often emotionally charged responses during conversations, and provides people with limited shared language proficiency a concrete tool for beginning to communicate. The inquiry, "Tell me about your job," accompanied by a picture of the learner's workplace or coworkers may lend itself to more spontaneous, revealing descriptions than the same question without a visual aid. Unlike conventional interviews in which workers may become self-conscious, irritated, or bored with repetitious probing questions, photo-sharing relieves people from the stress of being the *subject* of the interrogation and instead positions them as the expert, explaining the pictures and telling their own stories spontaneously (Collier & Collier, 1967/1986).

Because creating photographs in the workplace is seldom encouraged and may even be forbidden, the world of work remains largely invisible except the photos carefully managed by the organization. Photography in the workplace is usually used to enforce the status quo through surveillance cameras, photo ID badges, time-motion studies, advertising, and public relations images. Workers can challenge the slick and impersonal images generated for publicity purposes by photographing the realities of their hard work and camaraderie as well as the segregation or less than optimal working conditions they may experience (Moore, 1991). By generating photos from the workers' viewpoints, workplace practices and conditions can be documented, discussed, and improved.

The traditional role of power and control in the photographer-subject relationship can be problematic. The aggression of photography as expressed by the terms "shooting" and "taking" is often perceived as an act of the powerful against the powerless. It is common to find documentary studies of relatively powerless groups, such as children, the disabled, and the poor, but very few of powerful groups (Prosser & Schwartz, 1998). In documentary photography, often "the powerful, the established, the male, the colonizer, typically portray the less powerful, less established, female and colonized" (Harper, 1998, p. 30). Low-literate workers have seldom had the opportunity to document their own lives photographically.

To understand the essence of workers' lives, the stories must be told by them in their own images and words, and not through the distorted lens of outsiders' perceptions. Photographic literacy projects provide access to the technology and techniques needed to create self-representative images and the opportunity for learners to show their everyday reality to others (Ewald & Lightfoot, 2001). Encouraging learners to create their own photographic images has been proven particularly useful cross-culturally where language alone falls short in conveying meanings. Photographs can be used as autobiographical artifacts in telling one's own story and finding voice. Critical literacy proponents have likewise encouraged learners to represent their worlds through their own words and not merely to echo those of the dominant culture. By providing people with the means to create images of themselves and their worlds, we gain understandings that are often missed in conventional communications. The generative themes workers create in conjunction with their autodocumentary photographs are valuable in creating a meaningful literacy curriculum.

USING PHOTOGRAPHY IN
LITERACY INSTRUCTION

The use of images in representing generative themes for purposes of literacy and language learning is not a new idea. Much of Paulo Freire's literacy work incorporated "codifications," artist's renderings of typical situations of the peasants (Freire & Macedo, 1998). Cynthia Sihabout's (1999) work with a Paraguayan literacy program used photographs taken by the researcher to illustrate themes generated by discussions with the participants. Auerbach (1992; 1996) described the use of students' photos in LEA (language experience approach) exercises in which the teacher acts as a scribe while the student tells a story. Iwanaga (1992) has used photos in a community-based ESL program by introducing her own photographs and those taken by her students as an impetus for writing captions and stories. Deborah Barndt (Barndt, Cristall, & marino, 1982; Barndt, 2001) encouraged immigrant women to juxtapose images of themselves with images of ideal women portrayed in magazines and billboards and assisted immigrant women in creating photostories about their experiences seeking employment.

The use of images projected in the classroom is a powerful technique for generating group discussion (Wein, 1977) and using photos is particularly recommended for capturing the interest of tired laborers after a long shift (Fernau, 1979). Vocational reading projects have involved learners in photographing and interviewing women about their jobs and built a curriculum around the themes elicited from these images such as "determination," "pride," and "hardworking" (Ellowitch, 1983). Ewald's (2001) literacy through photography projects provide excellent examples of how writing skills can be enhanced by creating photographic images. Encouraging learners to create their own images and to analyze the images created by others are valuable ways of expanding literacies. These ideas and practices have opened new opportunities for the ways in which workplace literacy can be reinvented.

Creating Visual Imagery

Building class activities around photography and creating ways of transferring learning outside of the classroom are important ways of enhancing literacy learning. There are countless unforeseen discussion topics and activities that emerge from learners' uses of visual images. I have provided a brief description of some ways to begin creating learner-generated photographs as an example rather than a strict recipe to be followed.

I often introduce the topic of photography to learners by showing photos of people working in factories and also sharing photos of my own family and myself at work. At the first class, each student is given a disposable camera and asked to document their lives in- and outside of work. I request that they "take pictures of the things that are important to you." I give basic directions on how to use the cameras, although on occasion my zeal to ensure that the cameras were operated properly led me to explain one time too many how to wind the film, turn on the flash, and snap the picture. "Teacher," one student interrupted with restrained exasperation. "I *know*. In my country we *have* cameras." The film can be developed commercially and I pho-

Figure 6.1 Woman at home

tocopy and enlarge the pictures on overhead transparencies that are projected on the wall for everyone to see clearly for class discussions. The initial response to using the cameras is frequently excitement and enthusiasm. Though the photos learners take are usually ordinary snapshots without artistic pretension, the discussions which ensue from these images are thoughtful and enlightening. The selection of subjects is often surprising and there may be sharp contrasts between the gritty images taken at work and the shots of proud and well-dressed people in their homes (Figure 6.1).

Although the high cost of photographic materials and processing is sometimes thought to make these types of projects too expensive for many programs, I found that the price of purchasing disposable cameras and film processing cost about $4 per student with two students sharing a camera, less than one-sixth of the price of our regular textbooks. Digital cameras or videotaping may also be very cost-effective options if the equipment is already available.

Using Visual Images

Learners may begin to use their photos for their own purposes: to initiate discussion about workplace inequalities and health and safety issues; sharing with family, friends, and co-workers; documenting important aspects of their lives; engaging in English conversations during taking and viewing of photos; and publishing their stories on the web and in booklets. The stories written about the pictures are sometimes narrative descriptions about interactions while taking the photo, pointing out problems or inequities at work, descriptions of personal possessions, family, and friends, or education.

Sharing their photos leads the students to generate the themes that they then expand through discussions and writing exercises. We often begin class with discussions of pictures displayed on overhead transparencies. I ask basic questions about the picture and then write key vocabulary words offered by the class on the image using a second transparency over the photograph. Open-ended questions allow learners to embark on unpredictable topics and can be used as a beginning for discussions about workers' photographs: Tell me about this photo. Who is this? What is she doing? What does this picture represent to you? Why is this important? How do you feel about this photo? What title would you give it? Through this process, in one class we generated a vocabulary list of 46 commonly used work words which I typed and distributed to the class. We later created picture dictionaries using photocopies of the pictures and writing appropriate vocabulary words next to each image. These resources were used as reference materials throughout the course. Photos work particularly well with the multilevel classes often found in the workplace. While beginners are learning the basic names of objects and action depicted in the photos, more advanced learners can discuss and write about the significance of the images and the themes they elicit.

An early writing exercise is for each class member to select one of his or her own photos and write a description of it. I collect these short essays and type them, making minimal spelling and grammatical changes in order to keep the students' own style intact. Next I photocopy all of the stories with their pictures and make them into booklets for everyone. They take turns reading their own stories about their jobs, families, and cultural experiences from the booklets, and we discuss them at length. These booklets may also be displayed on the company bulletin board for all employees to read, and often workers from other areas stop by our classroom to remark how much they liked the essays and pictures. It is heartening for learners to see their own language progress as stories became longer and more descriptive in each book during the course.

There are many other activities that can be built around learner-generated photos.

Suggested Activities for Learner-Generated Photographs

- Work portraits: Pictures of yourself and other people working.
- Work environment: Places and objects at work including work areas, machines, tools, lunchrooms, and so on.
- Family and friends: Pictures of family members and friends outside of work.
- Favorite possessions: Pictures of your home, car, or collections.
- Leisure activities: Pictures of parties, fishing ponds, parks, and playgrounds.
- Community: Schools, neighborhoods, and grocery stores.
- What is important in my life: Photograph what is important to you.
- Reality vs. dream job: Show what your job is like now and how you would like it to be.
- Interview: Photograph and interview a person that the class should know about.
- Reality vs. advertising: Analyze advertising photos of stereo-

types or unrealistic images and create your own realistic images as a contrast.

- Photo-book and essays: Stories accompanied by pictures.
- Photo-dictionary: Document job-specific terms, slang, or difficult words.
- Sources of pride: Things you want to show off.
- Sources of concern: Things you want to improve.
- Photo-stories: Reenact experiences that happened to you and created a sequence of photographs accompanied by your own text to explain the story.

Learners are often proud of their photographs, eagerly showing them to their coworkers, spouses, and children. Many also send their photos to friends and relatives in their native countries. Sharing photos with the office staff and coworkers can become a starting point for social communication, while taking photos of others allows them to initiate and control English-language conversations. Photos engage people from many areas of the company in discussion with the learners. While taking pictures, learners usually explain their task, ask permission, and often seek a smile from their intended subject. After the pictures are developed, they may show them around the company. Photos become an easy way of engaging in social conversation and interacting with coworkers from other departments or different language backgrounds. Learners who may be shy, or reticent about speaking to strangers and exploring new areas often find a new confidence behind the camera lens as they learn to approach and address others. (See Figure 6.2.)

At one company, learners' pictures frequently depicted smiling coworkers and family members and proud documentation of their homes, cars, and children. They showed a sense of camaraderie inside the workplace and rewards outside. The subjects of the photographs were sometimes unexpected and telling. One woman took only photos of the framed photographs of her family hanging on the walls of her home. Another man took only photos of his long drive home from work through the windshield. Some people took pictures of their family members sleeping, as this was the only time they were able to see their

Figure 6.2 Man Operating Machine

spouses and children after work during the week (Figure 6.3). Several photographs were taken by immigrants inside bathrooms and were remarked upon by the American workers, "Well, you don't often see *that*."

Photos may generate discussions about company policies. In one company several photos showed workers punching in and out on the time clock and raised issues about pay docking, the practice of cutting workers' pay by 15 minutes if they punch in even 1 minute late (Figure 6.4).

One woman took separate photos of the parking lot for office employees and the factory parking lot to highlight the discrepancies between them:

> In this picture, this is the parking lot for the office. I like this parking lot, it is beautiful. Around the parking lot are the trees. Next to the parking lot is the Plasti-Co company. I am working in Plasti-Co a long time. I am not parking here because this parking lot is not for [hourly] employees. When I take this picture I remember I can not park here. If I park here I can sign the warning.

Figure 6.3 Child sleeping

Of the plant parking lot she wrote:

> This is the parking lot for [hourly] employees. In the parking lot
> it is dirty. Before, one temporary person parked on the ramp. He
> drove his car off the side of the ramp. His car went over. Russell
> and some people helped push it up. The company says: No em-
> ployees parking on ramp.

People with little power, money, or status seldom have their
opinions sought or heard by those in power. Caroline Wang explains:

> —to photograph their own lives therefore has a double power:
> it records for future generations what is happening in their lives
> now, and it enables them to define for themselves and others, in-
> cluding policy makers, what is worth remembering and what
> needs to be changed (Wang, 1995, p. 118).

Feminist approaches to photography have long been concerned with the political purposes of deconstructing media stereo-
types of women, and people of color, and reconstructing depic-

Figure 6.4 Time clock

tions of these groups by the subjects themselves. The creation of photographic representations which call attention to discrimination and other social issues that adversely impact less powerful groups and the creation of real, positive images to counteract the superficial pictures so often created by journalists and advertisers are important. Feminist photographic approaches begin with raising awareness of the ideological messages inherent in the bombardment of visual images encountered daily that shape our attitudes. "If we are shown enough pictures of women's bodies, or packets of Daz [soap], then we could probably conclude that society has a value for such imagery. Equally, if we *don't* see certain aspects of society then we could conclude that their omission (if we even notice it) is because they are of no importance." (Spence, 1995, p. 37–38).

Whether they are women, poor, or people of color, literacy students can find stereotypical images of their group portrayed in mainstream media that can be used as the basis of class discussion and projects. Viewing photos created by other people who share the learners' background can help to clarify these issues. Photographers such as Yong Soon Min (1995) an Asian American woman, describe their experiences visually. The images she creates are often overlaid with the stereotypic phrases she battles: "mama san," "miss saigon," "mail-order bride," "model minority," and "exotic immigrant." By countering the dual discrimination she faces as a woman and immigrant with powerful imagery and words, she is able to raise the awareness of viewers to her predicament. Workers may also create emotionally charged photographs showing the stresses of work including segregation and women's "double days" working in both paid and domestic labor. In this way they may use the power of photographs to correct imbalances in stereotypical representations (Soe, 1995).

In some ESL classes, participants added to discussions by bringing in photos and letters from home to aid telling their stories while others wrote essays and family histories. By using family photographs as an impetus for sharing stories and starting conversations, we learned how to see connections between past and present experiences. Learners also began to relate current struggles to succeed in a new country and learn a new language with past achievements, both personal and familial. One woman transcribed her entire photo storybook in phonetic Vietnamese and shared it with the other Vietnamese speakers. Others wrote their family histories and asked to have them typed up so that they could share them with their children. One brought in pictures of her vacation in Vietnam and her sister's wedding. Some also brought photo albums in addition to the usual sharing of wallet-kept family photos. One woman wrote of these photo-sharing experiences, "I learn many new words in the pictures."

Other Methods of Creating Visual Images

Many learners who struggle at first with traditional literacy activities of writing and reading have the opportunity to shine as artists and storytellers as they depict their world in more comfortable ways. Drawing, painting, and videotaping are other ways of creating images that can be examined and shared to improve literacy. Drawing is one of the simplest ways of using visual imagery in the classroom. Drawing can be introduced in a nonthreatening manner by the instructor's examples of simple stick figures. I usually draw a picture of myself teaching a class and learners laugh at my renderings, while feeling more at ease with their own drawing abilities. Learners are often enthused by the opportunity to draw pictures of themselves, coworkers, and work areas while explaining the work processes and caricatures they have created.

Videotaping can also be an easy-to-use tool for documenting situations and interviewing people at work. Seeing examples of real-life speech and body language replete with the stammering, overlaps, colloquialisms, ambient noise, and unfinished thoughts encountered in speaking, which differ from written and scripted language use, make excellent lessons. Watching themselves on tape can also be an accurate, if sometimes uncomfortable, way of attaining feedback about their speaking habits. Workers may also wish to create and tape skits to demonstrate good and bad communicative practices to share with coworkers.

Incorporating Computer Learning

Computers may become a focal point of class discussions and writings. In one ESL class learners often mentioned that they would like to learn about computers. Though few had ever used a computer themselves, some had purchased them for their children to use and were curious about how to use them. This led to discussions of computers and the interactive web exercise featuring their pictures and writing. Several of the students had Internet access at home and I put a number of their photos and essays along with interactive writing exercises on a web page so that they could show them to their families at home. These included grammar-based exercises that some students requested as well as comprehension questions and free-writing essays which could be submitted to me via e-mail. They enjoyed sharing their stories with their families through this novel method. Seeing their own pictures and stories on the strange medium of the Internet gave a sense of comfort and familiarity to a potentially intimidating new experience.

We also hooked up a computer in the classroom so that each person could have the experience of "surfing the net" by using our website as well as several first-language and English-learning sites. Most had never touched a keyboard or mouse before and there was a lot of nervous laughter as they attempted to find the right letters and move the cursor around the screen. They were interested in trying e-mail, learning about the costs of computer hardware and service providers, and talking about games and other uses of computers. Learning how to scan their images, write up their stories, and print them from the computer are useful skills in technology that may be learned through these projects. Students gain confidence through such experiences and supervisors often report transference of these skills to the job with significant gains in workers' comfort levels with technology at work.

Publishing and Exhibiting Learners' Images

Discovering ways in which learners' photographs and stories can be displayed and used to effect improvements within the workplace enhances the experience of creating visual images. Mounting and creating galleries of workers' images within the company, creating murals, publishing booklets of learners' photo-essays, and utilizing the Internet as means of creating further interactive learning environments are powerful methods of displaying the knowledge learners have made.

An exhibition of learners' photos and artwork in the workplace is an excellent way of promoting the program as well as staging workers' talents and viewpoints. It also provides an opportunity to recruit new students and to educate workers throughout the organization about language learning and literacy. Local galleries, libraries, schools, or banks may also be venues available for exhibitions. Creating a mural, quilt, or mosaic of learners' photos can brighten up the workplace and offer workers a shared sense of ownership and pride. It allows co-workers throughout the organization to see and understand the perspectives of their fellow employees.

However, knowing that their photos are going to be viewed by others, including supervisors, learners are may be uncharacteristically positive in their assessments of their jobs. One woman wrote for a photo book:

> The factory is very interesting, it has many people working because the work is important. Only the summer is hot, for in winter it is good. It is very big and very nice. I like to work every day. I'm learning new jobs thanks to my supervisor because he is very intelligent.

But in a more private setting she admitted, "I feel nervous when my supervisor watching me." Others are open with both the good and bad aspects of their jobs. One learner wrote, "I like my job because the people are friendly and I don't like it because the work is hard." Balancing both the positives and "opportunities" of the workplace when sharing learners' viewpoints publicly can be an interesting decision for learners to discuss and determine with their class.

Creating a class newsletter, fliers, posters, and writing stories accompanied by photos for local newspapers, company newsletters, or new reader publications are other ways of getting learners' viewpoints out to a wider audience. Encouraging workers to take up cameras for themselves in order to depict their own worldview is an important source of empowerment.

Putting cameras in the hands of the "undocumented" worker reverses the roles and allows workers to decide what should be documented photographically and how. Projects in which workers create their own representational images and accompanying texts are powerful examples of visual literacy used for self-expression. Such visual imagery projects serve to engage learners intellectually, encourage dialogues, bridge barriers of language, culture, and class differences, raise awareness of the program for those outside the program, and reinforce learning by fostering empowerment and authentic communication.

CHAPTER 7

Program Assessment and Evaluation

Assessments are used to improve the effectiveness of programs for the learners and to demonstrate the value of the program to the organization, funders, and other potential participants. Several groups benefit from accurate program evaluations. First, the learners are able to see how much they have learned and to receive recognition of their achievements. The instructors and educational providers can learn where the program has succeeded and how it may be improved. The organization and funders see the various ways in which their investments in time and money have paid off. Additionally program evaluation reports may serve to recruit new participants and bolster employee and public relations.

A truly learner-centered program uses meaningful program assessment that goes beyond standardized test scores. Evaluation should be collaborative and integrated throughout the program. By asking learners about their own goals and tracking their progress toward those goals, assessments become most effective. While outsiders may be interested in the fact that learners' reading skills have improved by 23% or that their math scores have gone up 1.3 grade levels, workers themselves may be more concerned with how this translates in their daily lives into getting work promotions, reading insurance information, and being able to help their children with schoolwork. Such real-life applications of learning are the true measures of program success.

The need for accountability and confidentiality are controversial issues in workplace literacy programs. When I conduct Spanish instruction or business writing classes the only evaluations given are smile sheets on which learners can note how they liked the class and whether they felt it was effective. In contrast, for basic skill classes, stringent documentation of post-test-score improvements and detailed reports of competency achievement are often required. This inconsistency and the treatment of basic skills learners as people who cannot be trusted with assessing their own learning should be examined. Standardized testing does not provide accountability to learners who deserve more than the bland and gummy oatmeal of the traditional reading skills covered in such tests served to them. Nor are funders and management who want to know that their money is making a difference in people's lives served by the sole use of such limited and lifeless evaluations. Subjecting low-level readers (who are not typically enthusiastic test takers) to a barrage of standardized assessments may also discourage program participation. They are also unlikely to reflect the learning of specialized and technical workplace vocabulary such as "sprue," or "micrometer" that workers are learning in their classes.

It is also necessary for educators to carefully consider the impact that their evaluations may have on learners' livelihoods and reputations on the job. Unlike the comparatively anonymous atmosphere of a college or community learning program, in the workplace, the perceived weaknesses of learners can quickly be spread through the company, leading to the possibilities of denied raises and promotions or even termination of employment. When reporting assessment results, consider the implications of the assessment, the confidentiality of the results, the possible exclusion of the employee from further training or promotion, and the impact on the learner's job security. It is important to respect participant confidentiality and to ensure that participants' individual progress reports are kept private, while aggregate class scores may be made available to management. An HR manager once asked me how a particular student was doing in class and I related that she sometimes seemed reluctant to participate. She was fired shortly after our conversation and I found that the information I had given was used as ammunition in building a case against her as a problem employee. Be aware that your casual comments can be hurtful and impact someone's livelihood. A broad smile and "Everyone is doing great" can be a way of deflecting muckraking inquiries targeting specific workers for punishment.

Most organizations are proud of their literacy programs and wish to promote awareness of them internally as well as throughout the community in order to emphasize the values of their organization. When this is the case, be sure to make the success of the program very visible company-wide and throughout the industry and community. Other organizations are more concerned with confidentiality, closed window classrooms, and preserving employees' privacy. They may not want customers to know about their low-literate or immigrant workforce or they may feel that there is shame and secrecy involved in literacy education. For these types of organizations, quieter and more private reports of program progress may be required.

However, secretive organizational attitudes may do more toward creating an atmosphere of shame and silencing than learners' own outlooks (Pharness, 2001). Workplace education provided for managers is rarely kept secret, nor are upper level workers regularly forced to take examinations to prove their learning in supervisory skills or time management techniques. This double standard and the treatment of literacy classes as something embarrassing or shameful and learners as untrustworthy should be questioned.

TYPES OF LEARNER-CENTERED ASSESSMENT

In order to make assessment both participatory and valid, it is important to use multiple assessments and to give learners a choice of assessments. There are myriad methods of assessing programs including post tests, competencies, portfolios, supervisor surveys, learner questionnaires, and other quantitative and qualitative measurements. Ensure that assessments are reflective of program activities. If most of the class activities focused on speaking skills, a pen and paper test is not the best choice. However, if class activities centered around workplace improvement projects, documentation of these projects and assessments of learner's abilities to perform literacy skills such as memo writing and introducing suggestions at meetings would be appropriate.

It is possible to use a combination of standardized and customized assessments to receive information about the impact of the classes. I often administer the Foreign Service Institute Language Proficiency Interview (FSI) assessment as a measure of oral language proficiency on the first and last days of an ESL class, or a customized reading test. Weekly quizzes of current vocabulary or grammar are popular with many learners. Supervisors may be given evaluation forms for each learner during the last week of classes and learners are usually given training impact surveys on the last day of class.

If workers have a goal of achieving a high score on a specific test in order to qualify for a promotion or get their GED, by all means spend the class time on test taking skills: filling in circles darkly and completely, making calculated guesses, and drilling tested vocabulary. However, if their goals are more in line with real-life tasks such as communicating at work, navigating the school system, reading important documents and getting better paying positions, focus on the evaluation of those tasks. We must either measure what they have learned or help them learn what will be measured. There is often little overlap between standardized tests of literacy and real world literacy, and the focus upon teaching only one may leave learners woefully unprepared for the other.

LEARNERS' ASSESSMENTS OF CLASSES

Learners' own assessments are the most important way to find out about their literacy learning and the successes and opportunities of the program. Discover what obstacles there are to program participation. Are the instruction methods and materials effective? What improvements can be made in the program? What goals have learners set and reached? Barriers and bridges to transferring learning from the classroom to the workplace must be explored and both the successes and challenges of the program should be uncovered in order to make improvements. Questionnaires, group discussions, surveys, and port-folios can all be used to gather such information. Learner self-assessments can also be done in one on one interviews or written in dialogue journals as an ongoing record and reflection upon their learning experiences. Assessments may be used at all stages of a program: initially as a diagnostic tool, during the program to measure the ongoing progress, and at the end to summarize achievements.

Group discussions of class outcomes can be particularly valuable. In one program learners brainstormed a list of things they liked about the English class which included: writing sto-ries, using the computer, reading, speaking about different cul-tures and countries, listening exercises, finding solutions to problems, corresponding in dialogue journals, and "everything." The list of things some learners wished to change about the class included less journaling, more vocabulary words, and wanting classes every day, rather than just twice a week. A drawback of using class discussion for evaluation is that learners may be hesi-tant to offer more suggestions for improving the classes for fear of hurting the instructor's feelings, despite the insistence that their input for class improvement is welcomed. Questionnaires can be also used for anonymity and to encourage learners who are reluctant to point out shortcomings of the program publicly.

Portfolios of learners' work and progress are another help-ful tool in assessing their learning. A portfolio can be as simple as a three-ring binder containing essays, letters, and other ex-amples of literacy activities the learner has accomplished. Going through learners' portfolios with them at the end of a course allows them to see their progress from the beginning to the end which may have happened so gradually that they are not aware of it. Many learners seem starved for praise in work environ-ments where their shortcomings are noticed more than their suc-cesses. "You say the first nice word for me in this company, in math class, 'Excellent'," one man wrote to me. Leafing through their work and seeing their improvements gives concrete evi-dence of their achievements. They may also wish to share selec-tions of their work publicly as a graduation speech, or on a poster as part of the evaluation reporting process.

Supervisor assessments can include questionnaires that ask about the impact of the program on their department and any difficulties which they have had with logistics such as covering work while learners are in class. It can also ask open-ended questions about the improvements they have observed in workers' performance. Table 7.1 shows a sample of results of supervisor surveys reporting the impact of participants completing an ESL program.

Customized post-tests of the actual documents and specific writing skills that learners have practiced are a natural, easy to prepare, and relatively painless testing choice. Post-tests can be oral, written, or activity based (for example, "Assemble this part according to instructions"). However, using standardized tests that incorporate low frequency vocabulary and skills that learners have not encountered in a reality-based program will give predictably poor results. We should ask if we are measuring learning and practical applications or are we measuring test taking skills. I am good at taking tests, and when I took a college placement exam that measured my ability to conjugate Spanish verbs I was placed into an upper level class with native speakers. I floundered in this atmosphere where the language was actually used because I had no practice with speaking beyond parroting memorized classroom dialogues. Despite my test scores, I did not really know how to use the language. Likewise, one of my reading students was an experienced and skilled forklift driver who was unable to pass his written certification exam. This disjuncture between the actual ability to perform and the ability to pass a test needs to be recognized and repaired. Learners must determine with their instructors the amount of time they wish to devote to drills on material that will be found on a standardized test and practicing exam taking strategies and balancing this with the need for more authentic learning activities.

While employers and funders may wish to view test scores to check learners' progress, the confidentiality of specific test scores should be maintained for the protection of employees' privacy. There are legal ramifications if employers choose to demote, punish, or exclude employees from further training based on test scores rather than job performance. For learners, seeing

Table 7.1 Supervisor Training Impact Survey

	Greatly Improved	Somewhat Improved	No Change	Not Applicable
Speaks English more often	22%	74%	4%	0%
Understands oral instructions and directions	26%	74%	0%	0%
Understands written instructions and directions	26%	65%	9%	0%
Completes work documents and forms correctly	22%	57%	22%	0%
Follows safety practices and rules	9%	74%	17%	0%
Communicates successfully without the need for translation	17%	61%	22%	0%
Understands and successfully performs workplace math	22%	74%	0%	4%
Works more productively and efficiently	0%	70%	30%	0%
Takes greater initiative on the job	0%	70%	26%	4%
Makes more suggestions or speaks up more in meetings	4%	57%	39%	0%
Deals successfully with workplace technology	0%	70%	26%	4%
Is ready for more advanced workplace training	4%	9%	87%	0%
Qualifies for promotion or transfer to preferred job	4%	9%	87%	0%

their own test scores may be of interest if they are truly reflective of their learning. Validation of learning through test results can be powerful and one learner broke into tears when she saw her excellent post-test reading score, "I *knew* I wasn't stupid," she cried angrily. Being told that we are stupid, lazy, or otherwise lacking are brands that are hard to remove. The opportunity to undo some of the emotional hurt that has been inflicted upon people in the name of education is an unproclaimed benefit of learner-centered literacy programs.

Helping employers to understand the meaning underlying test scores is essential. One company wished to publicly recognize the employee who had shown the greatest improvement on his reading test score. However, the 700% improvement was a result of going from getting one answer right to getting eight right, though this was still less than his chances of guessing randomly on a 40 point test. Educators must explain the reasoning behind the scores and interpret results for those who want to know grade-level equivalencies. Using grade levels as measurement for adults is both demeaning and misleading. Being told that you read at a lower level than the average 9-year-old is hurtful and not a true reflection of the other knowledge and skills that workers possess. There is also the danger that employers who hear that their key employees can now read at a seventh-grade level after participating in a literacy program will interpret this as a sign of their deficiency rather than success.

Competencies are another popular means of assessing progress in workplace literacy programs. Competency reports are listings of specific skills with an assessment of whether or not the learner has mastered the skill adequately. Learners may wish to identify competencies they would like to achieve at the beginning of the course and to add new ones as the class continues. Some examples of competencies may be "Correctly fills out an accident report form," "Communicates ideas verbally at meetings," "Reads and creates flow charts," or "Reads 401K brochure to select retirement options."

Quantitative measurements can be made of any information the organization keeps statistics for: safety, productivity, promotions, scrap, on-time delivery, absences, return on investment, tardiness, production rate, suggestion box submissions, turnover, disciplinary action, and so forth. For example, at one company recorded accidents were reduced from 12 the previous year down to 3, and management credited the ESL classes with favorably impacting the accident rate through the emphasis on reading safety signs and, documents and promoting understanding of safety procedures. One Human Resources manager regularly utilized the literacy class as a way to explain difficult policies such as the HMO and PPO health plans and 401k investments, and she measured the success of the program by the amount of hours saved each week from employees coming to the office and asking for policy explanations. Counting the number of promotions and pay raises earned by participants is another powerful measurement.

Many qualitative measurements can be made more concrete and quantitative by the use of surveys. By asking "What have been the changes you have seen as a result of this program?" and tallying the results of supervisors and coworkers as well as learners, a clearer understanding of program impact may be obtained. Outcomes such as building morale, self-esteem, and community within the organization, providing more opportunity for upward mobility at work, increased job performance, safety awareness, and productivity, decreased reliance on translators, and enhanced understanding of company policies are all valuable indicators that can be measured through surveys.

TRANSER OF LEARNING

Transfer of learning is a key goal in learner-centered programs. Immediately being able to apply the language they learn in class to pragmatic situations such as making appointments, talking to schoolteachers, conversing with coworkers about photos and changes in the workplace, using the Internet, and writing checks allows practice which reinforces and builds confidence in their literacy skills.

Find out how workers have adapted to and changed the environment of their workplace. What can participants do now that they could not do before at work, at home, and in their communities? What further education are they participating in? Many learners will begin to attend community college classes after succeeding in workplace classes. What are the outcomes and impact of a learner-centered program? Have there been changes in job performance, self-esteem, improvements in reading, writing, and math skills? In what ways does gaining confidence in written and spoken English in the classroom translate into a greater sense of empowerment in other aspects of learners' lives?

The frequent comment, "Now we have more English," suggests that learners have gained possession of a valuable commodity, which can be used and exchanged for tangible perks such as workplace improvements, insurance information, and doctor's appointments. The empowerment learners gain through the changes they made in their workplace, their improved communication skills, building community with coworkers, critically reflecting on their situations, and producing knowledge through their discussions and writings provides opportunities for bettering their lives in and outside of work. Teachers may wish to keep their own daily journal about learners' progress as a record of learning. Documenting learners' increased involvement in work committees, schools, and faith-based or civic organizations is just one example of how to demonstrate that their learning is being transferred for practical applications.

While some of the changes that take place as a result of literacy classes are primarily useful to workers, such as communicating about their children's education or getting new microwave ovens in the lunchroom, and others are primarily advantageous to management, such as improved productivity and on-time delivery, the majority of program outcomes are benefits that are shared by both the company management and workers such as increased safety awareness, comfort with technology, improved communication, and higher morale. This provides incentives for company management to continue providing the program without centering the outcomes of the curriculum solely upon the mandates set by the employer. The empowering aspects of critical reflection, communication, community building, creation of knowledge, and change making can provide avenues of learning that are meaningful for workers while offering genuine benefits to their employers.

REPORTING RESULTS

The ways in which the company, workers, and community alike benefit from programs can be shown through effective reporting and presentation of evaluation results. In order to garner the support of management, try to use their own language and metaphors in reporting results, whether terms of industrial productivity or customer-centered service jargon. Translating successes from educational terminology such as "Successfully writes sentences with subject verb agreement" into business ones such as "Clearly conveys customer requests in writing" are important details which aid in program understanding. Reporting can be a great opportunity for public relations as well as for recruiting potential students and for recognizing learners' achievements. There are many innovative ways of reporting program evaluations, including presentations, graduation parties, video clips, galleries, and web pages.

Methods of Reporting Assessment Results

- Have learners create and deliver a PowerPoint presentation of what they have learned and accomplished with their improved literacy.
- Create a video montage of learners and coworkers commenting about program outcomes.
- Record a compact disk of learners reading their stories aloud.
- Present a gallery or mural displaying learners' photographs and written work.
- Post program successes on the company or class web page.
- Make an announcement to the local paper.
- Encourage learners to write letters to the CEO, grant provider, HR director, or other involved parties describing the impact of the class.
- Publish an article in the company newsletter.
- Show results in a report.
- Have participants tell their own stories in a memo or class newsletter.
- Perform a skit, live or videotaped, to show the outcomes of the program. Learners can write and memorize their parts.
- Throw a big graduation ceremony. Invite managers and coworkers.

- Document workplace improvement projects in words and photos. For example: "These new ventilation fans were installed through a suggestion by the Essential Skills class."
- Create graphs showing the quantitative impact of program.

Documenting the transformations based upon the problems and concerns depicted in learners' photographs and stories and providing venues for learners to share accounts of their successes may serve as important evaluation tools. Implementing workplace improvement projects and showing financial benefits to the company through improved safety, increased productivity, and diminished turnover are valuable. A participatory curriculum might encourage learners to discuss and improve workplace conditions, and speak up about their job concerns. Additionally, their communication skills, morale, and awareness of safety at work may show marked improvements. Good evaluation tools serve to make these improvements visible both to learners and other program stakeholders.

One way to show results is in a book or display of photo-essays. One woman wrote: "I like Plasti-Co Molding, they help our employees learn more English . . . I have a lot of friends at class, we work together, so many different accents." Another man wrote about his picture of the class, "Here is the classroom, this place was improvised by the molding company so this way the molding workers can take the English classes. All of us are thankful to the company for giving us the opportunity to learn English." Another learner wrote below a picture she took of the class: "I sit in class. I study English ESL with my friends. This here is my teacher at the table with my friends. We take pictures. We are happy. I love it."

Don't underestimate the value of the fuzzy, heartwarming anecdote in relating program results in addition to cold hard numbers. The success stories of learners who now have the confidence to read on their own, to apply for promotions, and to help their families and communities are remembered long after the statistics of reading score improvements have faded. One manager told me he would continue to offer more ESL classes because workers were now saying hello and engaging him in conversations whereas before they had avoided making eye contact. Learners' letters thanking management or relating personal successes can be very powerful. Testimonials and anecdotes such as "Now I can help my kids with homework, now I can participate more in departmental meetings," or "Now I am going on to get my GED" are valuable outcomes of a successful program and should be documented.

Reports by managers and coworkers are valued as well. One engineer reported that his coworkers are now more relaxed when they are talking in English and that they attempt to do so more frequently. A quality manager reported that communication "has improved quite a bit, I'm impressed with what the program has accomplished. Now the operators ask me to make corrections in their English when they speak. This is very promising, it shows that they want to learn." Collecting such testimonies on paper or in a video montage can have great impact.

It is essential to report the changes that have been made as a result of feedback or to address why they have not. This shows involved parties that their voices are heard and valued. A simple announcement such as, "We changed the class time to accommodate supervisors' production schedules and we are using a new dictionary with larger print to meet learners' requests" informs everyone of the program's awareness and sensitivity to the needs of all stakeholders.

RECOGNITION

Low-literate workers seldom hold jobs where they receive a great deal of respect and recognition. Publicly acknowledging the progress they have made with ceremonies, certificates, parties, and newsletter write-ups can be especially validating experiences for them. Tangible rewards such as a promotion, pay raise, parking privileges, gift certificates, bonuses, or even the changing of a job title are significant ways of recognizing workers' achievements after successful completion of a class. It is also important to provide them with certificates of achievement as a record of their participation. Many basic skills learners have had their certificates framed and displayed in a place of honor in their homes.

A large celebration of the literacy class graduation demonstrates that education and training are valued by the company. Some students have never participated in a graduation ceremony before and are elated at the opportunity to do so. One class even brought in caps and gowns to wear during graduation. Some companies provide a cake emblazoned with "Congratulations, Graduates," and the president, supervisors, and managers attend to wish the learners well. Learners often express gratitude for the literacy classes at these events. During a graduation party one Vietnamese woman very nervously announced that she would like to thank the president and the company for the ESL classes. She made an impromptu short speech, relating that she had learned a lot during the class and was very grateful. Her announcement was rewarded with a round of applause from coworkers. Such celebrations generate further enthusiasm for the program and bolster morale for learners and coworkers alike. Successful program assessment ensures that learning does not end with the evaluation but is reconfigured and renewed into even better opportunities. In this way, we can ensure quality, learner-centered education that promotes communication and understanding in the workplace and beyond.

CONCLUDING THOUGHTS

The world of work is a familiar yet complex place. It is the site where we spend many of our waking hours, where we form friendships and find satisfaction, express our talents, face frustrations, and are educated both informally and formally. We learn to read the faces and intonations of supervisors, and to read the tensions and territorial boundaries delineated by our fellow employees. We interpret the organizational customs and rituals that complement or contrast with written policies. We grow as we become more experienced in reading words and reading the world. We struggle, working through our imperfections, our crooked letters, and our broken communications toward understanding and wholeness.

The marriage of business and literacy education is an unusual but potentially satisfying one. Worker-centered literacy can begin to change notions of what it means to be literate in the workplace, to enhance organizational communication at many levels, and to enlighten coworkers as it expands traditional expectations. By building problem-posing and critical-thinking skills, workers learn ways of transforming instead of merely adapting to their workplaces.

Learner-centered programs allow us to create small pockets of community and hope in our work that can catalyze positive communication practices that reach farther from our classroom than we might imagine. They allow learners to define themselves by their potential rather than their past or preconceptions. Learner-centered approaches are both practical and effective. They start where learners are, use the talents they already have, and encourage them to do more. They help organizations by implementing improvements in communication, quality, and productivity, reinforcing learning through practical applications, and creating cooperative environments where morale and performance can soar.

When I recently asked my ESL class what advice they had for helping others to learn English they replied, "Don't be afraid." Fear of the unknown, of embarrassment, misunderstanding, looking foolish, or being put down keep us tethered to familiar ground. Taking risks in which our successes are encouraging and our mistakes are often less lethal than we feared brings the confidence needed to continue striding forward. Learner-centered programs provide the safe and fertile environment in which this confidence can begin to grow.

Learner-centered literacy is not only engaging but also empowering. It helps workers to examine work relationships from a new perspective, looking at power structures and communicative practices with an eye to improve them. It provides opportunities for innovation and renewal and it encourages us to live out our lives and dreams more fully with integrity and hope.

Like most worthwhile endeavors, it is not always easy. Innovation may be met with resistance, and budding empowerment can be callously trod upon. Yet there is hope even for the most inflexible and bureaucratic organizations because they are made up of the individual building blocks of human beings with souls and dreams, with the desire to create a good greater than themselves and to find meaning in their work, for whom business is not only business. Each time we choose to enhance understanding at work through honest communication, we have scored a small victory that may cause far-reaching ripples. Not in some far off and utopian future, but right here and now, using what we have, to do what we can.

REFERENCES

Askov, E., & Aderman, B. (1991). Understanding the history and definitions of workplace literacy. In M. C. Taylor, G. R. Lewe, & J. A. Draper (Eds.), *Basic skills for the workplace* (pp. 7–20). Toronto: Culture Concepts Inc.

Auerbach, E. (1990). Toward a transformative model of worker education: A Freirean perspective. In S. H. London, E. R. Tarr, & J. F. Wilson (Eds.), *The re-education of the American working class* (pp. 225–238). Westport, CT: Greenwood Press.

Auerbach, E. (1992). *Making meaning, making change: Participatory curriculum development for adult ESL literacy.* McHenry, IL: Center for Applied Linguistics and Delta Systems, Inc.

Auerbach, E. (1996). *Adult ESL/literacy from the community to the community: A guidebook for participatory literacy training.* Mahwah, NJ: Lawrence Erlbaum Associates, Inc.

Auerbach, E., & Wallerstein, N. (1987). *ESL for action: Problem-posing at work.* Reading, MA: Addison-Wesley.

Barndt, D. (1980). *Education and social change: A photographic study of Peru.* No city listed: Kendall/Hunt Publishing Co.

Barndt, D. (2001). Naming, making, and connecting—reclaiming lost arts: The pedagogical possibilities of photo-story production. In P. Campbell & B. Burnaby (Eds.), *Participatory practices in adult education* (pp. 31–54). Mahwah, NJ: Lawrence Erlbaum Associates.

Barndt, D., Cristall, F., & marino, d. (1982). *Getting there: Producing photostories with immigrant women.* Toronto: Between the Lines.

Beck, R. (1996). *The case against immigration: The moral, economic, social and environmental reasons for reducing U.S. immigration back to traditional levels.* New York: W. W. Norton & Company.

Bouchard, P. (1998). Training and work: Myths about human capital. In S. M. Scott, B. Spencer, & A. M. Thomas (Eds.), *Learning for life: Canadian readings in adult education* (pp. 188–199). Toronto: Thompson Educational Publishing, Inc.

Bowe, J., Bowe, M., & Streeter, S. C. (Eds.). (2000). *Gig: Americans talk about their jobs at the turn of the millenium.* New York: Crown Publishing.

Boyle, M.-E. (1999). Immigrant workers and the shadow education system. *Educational policy, 13*(2 May), 251–279.

Boyle, M.-E. (2001). *The new schoolhouse: Literacy, managers and belief.* Westport, CT: Praeger.

Bureau of Labor Statistics. (2001a). *Occupations with the largest job growth, 2000–2010.* Available: *http://www.bls.gov/emp/emptab4. htm* [2002, August 13].

Bureau of Labor Statistics. (2001b). *Report on the American Workforce: 2001.* Available: www.bls.gov.

Canadian Labour Congress. (1999). *Making it clear: Clear language for union communications.* Ottawa: Canadian Labour Congress.

Canadian Labour Congress. (2000). *Bargaining basic skills: What unions should know about negotiating worker-centered literacy programs.* Ottawa: Canadian Labour Congress.

Canadian Labour Congress. (2001). *Seeds for change: A curriculum guide for worker-centered literacy.* Ottawa: Canadian Labour Congress.

Chaney, B. M. (1994). *Application of adult education principles to workplace literacy program descriptions.* Unpublished doctoral dissertation, Ohio State University.

Claire, E. (1998). *Dangerous English 2000: An indispensable guide for language learners and others.* McHenry, IL: Delta Systems.

Collier, J. J., & Collier, M. (1967/1986). *Visual anthropology: Photography as a research method.* Albuquerque: University of New Mexico Press.

Collins, S. (1989), Workplace literacy: Corporate tool or worker empowerment? Social Policy 20(1), 26–30.

Cunningham, P. (1993). The politics of worker's education: Preparing workers to sleep with the enemy. *Adult Learning, 5*(1), 13–14,24.

Cushman, E. (1999). Critical literacy and institutional language. *Research in the Teaching of English, 33*(3), 245–275.

DeFoe, T., & Farrell, R. (2001). *More learning on the shop floor.* Paper presented at the Sixth Annual Workplace Learning Conference, Chicago.

Defoe, T. A., Belfiore, M. E., Folinsbee, S., Hunter, J., & Jackson, N. (2001). *Situating literacy in the workplace.* Paper presented at the Second International Conference on Researching Work and Learning, Calgary.

Demetrion, G. (2000). *Literacy for life: Life application curriculum sourcebook lessons*. Literacy Volunteers of America. Available: *http://www.crec.org/atdn/teacher_*resources/lvalifeapp.shtml [2000, March 26].

Ehrig, G. (2001). On facing phoney baloney. *Our Times, 20*(4), 52.

Elish-Piper, L. (2000). An analysis of the social-contextual responsiveness of adult education in urban family literacy programs: Trends, obstacles, and solutions. *Reading research and Instruction, 39*, 184–200.

Elish-Piper, L. (2002). Adult literacy. In B. Guzetti (Ed.), *Literacy in America: An Encyclopedia of History, Theory, and Practice* (pp. 19–22). Santa Barbara, CA: ABC Clio.

Ellowitch, A. (1983). *A curriculum in employment: Women and the world of work*. Philadelphia: Lutheran Settlement House Women's Program.

English Literacy and Civics Education Project. (2001). *What to do if you are stopped by the police*. 30 Harvard Street, Worcester, MA: Lutheran Community Services of Southern New England, Refugee and Immigrant Services.

Ewald, W., & Lightfoot, A. (2001). *I wanna take me a picture: Teaching photography and writing to children*. New York: Beacon Press.

Fernau, C. N. (1979). *The use of photographs in workers' education: An instructional aid for workers' educators and trade unionists*. Geneva, Switzerland: International Labour Office.

Fingeret, H. (1994). Politics and power in workplace literacy education. *Educational Researcher, 23*(9), 31.

Fingeret, H. A., & Drennon, C. (1997). *Literacy for life: Adult learners, new practices*. New York: Teachers College Press.

Folinsbee, S. (2000). *Looking back, looking forward: A conversation with workplace educators*. Tri En Communications. Available: http://www.nald.ca/fulltext/lookback/looking.pdf [2001, December 1].

Ford, D. (1992). Toward a more literate workforce. *Training & Development, 46*(11 Nov.), 52–55.

Freire, A. M. A., & Macedo, D. (Eds.). (1998). *The Paulo Freire reader*. New York: Continuum.

Freire, P. (1973/1993). *Pedagogy of the oppressed* (Myra Bergman Ramos, Trans.). (20th Anniversary ed.). New York: The Continuum Publishing Company.

Freire, P. (1996). *Letters to Cristina* (Donaldo Macedo, Trans.). New York: Routledge.

Freire, P., & Macedo, D. (1987). *Literacy: Reading the word and the world*. South Hadley, MA: Bergin & Garvey.

Gallo, M. L. (2001). *From the shadows to the light: Learning to read the world of work through photography*. Unpublished doctoral dissertation, Northern Illinois University, DeKalb, IL.

Gee, J. P., Hull, G., & Lankshear, C. (1996). *The new work order: Behind the language of the new capitalism*. Boulder, CO: Westview Press.

Gilmore, P. (1992). "Gimme room": School resistance, attitude, and access to literacy. In P. Shannon (Ed.), *Becoming political: Readings and writings in the politics of literacy education* (pp. 113-127). Portsmouth, NH: Heinemann.

Giroux, H. A. (1992). Critical literacy and student experience: Donald Graves' approach to literacy. In P. Shannon (Ed.), *Becoming political: Readings and writings in the politics of literacy education* (pp. 15-20). Portsmouth, NH: Heinemann.

Goldstein, T. (1997). *Two languages at work: Bilingual life on the production floor*. (Vol. 74). Berlin/New York: Mouton de Gruyter.

Gowen, S. G. (1992). *The politics of workplace literacy: A case study*. New York: Teachers College Press.

Gowen, S. G., & Bartlett, C. (1997). Friends in the kitchen. In G. Hull (Ed.), *Changing work, changing workers: Critical perspectives on language, literacy, and skills* (pp. 141-158). Albany: State University of New York Press.

Haas, T., Smoke, T., & Hernandez, J. (1991). A collaborative model for empowering nontraditional students. In S. Benesch (Ed.), *ESL in America: Myths and possibilities* (pp. 112-130). Portsmouth, NH: Boyton/Cook Publishers.

Harper, D. (1998). An argument for Visual Sociology. In J. Prosser (Ed.) *Image-based research: A sourcebook for qualitative researchers* (pp. 24-41). Bristol, PA: Fallmer Press.

Hull, G. (Ed.). (1997a). *Changing work, changing workers: Critical perspectives on language, literacy, and skills*. Albany, NY: State University of New York Press.

Hull, G. (1997b). Hearing other voices: A critical assessment of popular views on literacy and work. In G. Hull (Ed.), *Changing work, changing workers: critical perspectives on language, literacy, and skills* (pp. 3-42). Albany: State University of New York.

Iwanaga, E. (1992). *The camera in the classroom: A description of the uses of photography in an adult ESL program with samples of student work*. Lynn, MA: Northeast SABES.

Joliffe, D. (1997). Finding yourself in the text: Identity formation in the discourse of workplace documents. In G. Hull (Ed.), *Changing work, changing workers: Critical perspectives on language, literacy and skills* (pp. 335–349). Albany: State University of New York Press.

Kaestle, C. F., Damon-Moore, H., Stedman, L. C., Tinsley, K., & Trollinger, W. V. J. (Eds.). (1991). *Literacy in the United States: Readers and reading since 1880*. New Haven: Yale University Press.

Kozol, J. (1992). *Savage Inequalities: Children in America's Schools*. NY: Harper Perennial.

Krashen, S. (2001). *Free voluntary reading: Still a great idea*. Paper presented at the Illinois TESOL/BE 28th Annual State Convention.

Krashen, S. D., & Terrell, T. D. (1983). *The natural approach: Language acquisition in the classroom*. Hayward, CA: Alemany Press.

Linder, P. E., & Elish-Piper, L. (1995). Listening to learners: Dialogue journals in a family literacy program. *Reading Research and Instruction: The Journal of the College Reading Association, Annual,* 313–325.

Mawer, G. (1999). *Language and literacy in workplace education: Learning at work*. London: Longman.

Milton, M. J. (1999). Perceptions about women's nonparticipation in workplace literacy courses. *Journal of Adolescent & Adult Literacy, 42*(5), 340–351.

Min, Y. S. (1995). deColonization. In D. Neumaier (Ed.), *Reframings: New American feminist photographies* (pp. 134–137). Philadelphia: Temple University Press.

Moore, C. (1991). *Indecent exposures: Twenty years of Australian feminist photography*. St. Leonards, NSW, Australia: Allen & Unwin.

Moore, R. (1999). Empowering the ESL worker within the new work order. *Journal of Adolescent & Adult Literacy, 43*(2), 142–152.

National Association of Manufacturers. (2002). *The Skills Gap 2001: Manufacturers confront persistent skills shortages in an uncertain economy*. Washington, D.C.: Anderson Center for Workforce Success.

O'Connor, P. (2000). Workers' texts, identities and learning possibilities in the smart workforce. In R. Gerber & C. Lankshear (Eds.), *Training for a smart workforce* (pp. 151–176). London: Routledge.

Paratore, J. R. (2001). *Opening doors, opening opportunities: Family literacy in an urban community*. Needham Heights, MA: Allyn & Bacon.

Pharness, G. (2001). From where we live, how far can we see? In P. Campbell & B. Burnaby (Eds.), *Participatory practices in adult education* (pp. 197–220). Mahwah, NJ: Lawrence Erlbaum Associates.

Prosser, J., Schwartz, D. (1998) Photographs within the sociological research process. In J. Prosser (Ed.), Image-based research: A sourcebook for qualitative researchers (pp. 24–41). Bristol, PA: Fallmer Press.

Purcell-Gates, V. (1995). *Other people's words: The cycle of low literacy*. Cambridge: Harvard University Press.

Purcell-Gates, V., & Waterman, R. A. (2000). *Now we read, we see, we speak: Portrait of literacy development in an adult Freirean-based class*. Mahwah, NJ: Lawrence Erlbaum Associates.

Quigley, B. A. (1993). Seeking a voice: Resistance to schooling and learning. *Adult Basic Education, 3*(2), 77–93.

Reimers, D. (1998). *Unwelcome strangers: American identity and the turn against immigration*. New York: Columbia University Press.

Rhoder, C. A., & French, J. N. (1994). Workplace literacy: From survival to empowerment and human development. *Journal of Reading, 38*(2), 110–120.

Roberts, C., Davies, E., & Jupp, T. (1992). *Language and discrimination: A study of communication in multi-ethnic workplaces*. London: Longman.

Rose, A. (1992). America at work: New partnerships for corporate America and education. *Adult Learning, 3*(8), 5.

Rosow, L. V. (1995). *In forsaken hands: How theory empowers literacy learners*. Portsmouth, MA: Heinemann.

Ryan, G. H. (1994). *Workplace literacy: How to get started—A guide for Illinois businesses*. Springfield, IL: Secretary of State Literacy Office.

Schultz, K. (1992). *Training for basic skills or educating workers?: Changing conceptions of workplace education programs*. Berkely, CA: National Center for Research in Vocational Education.

Shannon, P. (1992). Reading instruction and social class. In P. Shannon (Ed.), *Becoming political: Readings and writings in the politics of literacy education* (pp. 128–138). Portsmouth, NH: Heinemann.

Sihabout, C. (1999). *A matter of courage: Experiences of participants in a Freirean adult literacy workshop in rural Paraguay*. Unpublished doctoral dissertation, Northern Illinois University, DeKalb, IL.

Soe, V. (1995). Turning the tables: Three Asian American artists. In D. Neumaier (Ed.), Reframings: New American feminist Photographies (pp. 262–271). Philadelphia: Temple University Press.

Spence, J. (1995). *Cultural sniping: The art of transgression*. London: Routledge.

Sum, A., Kirsch, I., & Taggart, R. (2002). *The twin challenges of mediocrity and inequality: Literacy in the U.S. from an international perspective*. Princeton: Educational Testing Service.

Szudy, E., & Arroyo, M. G. (1994). *The right to understand: Linking literacy to health and safety training*. Berkeley, CA: Labor Occupational Health Program, University of California.

Terkel, S. (1997). *Working: People talk about what they do all day and how they feel about what they do*. NY: New Press.

Thorn, I. (2001). Literacy is a labour issue. In M. C. Taylor (Ed.), *Adult literacy now* (pp. 123–136). Toronto: Culture Concepts, Inc.

Wallerstein, N. (1983). *Language and culture in conflict: Problem-posing in the ESL classroom*. Reading, MA: Addison-Wesley.

Wang, C. (1995). Self-portraits by village women. In W. K. Yi, V. C. Li, Z. W. Tao, Y. K. Lin, M. A. Burris, W. Y. Ming, X. Y. Yun, & C. Wang (Eds.), *Visual voices: 100 photographs of village China by the women of Yunnan province*. Yunnan, China: Yunnan People's Publishing House.

Wein, J. (1977). *The big picture: Photography and slides in the classroom*. Waitsfield, VT: Vermont Crossroads Press.

Yaffe, D., & Williams, C. L. (1998). Why women chose to participate in a family literacy program and factors that contributed to the program's success. *Journal of Adolescent and Adult Literacy, 42*, 8–19.

INDEX